£4

THE BALKANS

THE BALKANS

A SHORT HISTORY FROM GREEK TIMES TO THE PRESENT DAY

BY
EDGAR HÖSCH

Translated by
TANIA ALEXANDER

FABER & FABER
3 QUEEN SQUARE
LONDON

First published in England 1972
by Faber & Faber Limited
3 Queen Square, London WC1
Revised edition with 9 extra maps
Printed in England by
Western Printing Services Ltd, Bristol

ISBN 0 571 09372 8

Originally published by
W. Kohlhammer GmbH. Stuttgart,
as
Geschichte der Balkanländer

CONTENTS

MAPS

Acknowledgement is due to *Westermanns Atlas zur Weltgeschichte* (Brunswick, 1963) for much of the information contained in maps 3–8, 10 and 11.

ACKNOWLEDGEMENTS FOR
ENGLISH EDITION

We should like to thank Dr. Muriel Heppell and Miss Phyllis Auty of the School of Slavonic and East European Studies, University of London, for the editorial assistance and advice they have kindly given us in the preparation of the English edition.

TRANSLATOR'S NOTE

Where names have an accepted English version this has been used. In all other cases, local spellings have been used.

INTRODUCTION

The multi-national complex of south-eastern Europe still has a singular attraction for the outside world. Hardly anybody fails to be charmed by its landscape and its confusing picture of juxtaposed nationalities, cultures, religions and social customs. Since the sensational literary discovery in the eighteenth century of the ancient 'lost' world of Balkan patriarchal society, a great deal of specialized research has been undertaken by scholars from many countries, which has added much to our knowledge of this neglected border region. Nevertheless, the south-eastern area of the European continent lying between the middle and lower reaches of the Danube and territory under Greek influence has remained a border region as far as historical studies of particular countries are concerned.

My object in writing this short book has been to help a wider circle of readers understand that unfamiliar part of Europe with its constantly changing history. The inevitable limitations of space and subject matter have made me conscious of two dangers: first, of offering inadequate summaries to my more knowledgeable readers, and second, of giving other readers who are anxious to learn more about the area, too rough a view and interpretation of complex events–providing them with little more than an unsatisfactory glimpse into such an inexhaustible kaleidoscope.

It has, however, been impossible to attempt anything more than an introduction to the eventful political history of the central Balkans. By describing the origin, formation and collapse of political systems through the centuries from ancient times to the present day, I have aimed at revealing the special problems of political organization in the region. As a result of its fatal geographical position, interposed between two major powers, it became the object of power politics to such an extent that it was prevented

9

from working out its own destiny. Again and again it was involved in the expansionist policies of mighty neighbouring countries. My desire to show the possibilities and limitations that have determined the overall history of south-eastern Europe has ruled out the inclusion of simple histories of individual nations or of a detailed analysis of the origins of modern and contemporary developments. The history of the area as a whole, as well as that of its protagonists–the Slovenes, Croats, Serbs, Bulgarians, Albanians and Romanians–can only be comprehended if it is viewed from the standpoint of world history, freed from the distortions of nationalism.

I

FOUNDATIONS AND FRAMEWORK

Maps of south-eastern Europe show three sovereign states in the central Balkans:

the Socialist Federal Republic of Yugoslavia (the S.F.R.J., or Socijalistička Federativna Republika Jugoslavija) with an area of 255,804 square kilometres and 19·7 million inhabitants (1966 census),

the Peoples' Republic of Bulgaria (the N.R.B., or Narodna Republika Bulgariya) with an area of 110,928 square kilometres and 8·2 million inhabitants (1965 census), and

the Peoples' Republic of Albania (the R.P.S.H., or Republika Popullore e Shqipërisë) with an area of 28,748 sqaure kilometres and 1·86 million inhabitants (1965 census).

On their southern frontiers are areas occupied by settlers of Greek origin who brought their culture with them; to the south-east is what remains of the European part of the former Ottoman Empire, that is, the areas around Istanbul and Edirne; and to the north-west and north are territories under Italian, Austrian and Hungarian sovereignty.

North of the middle and lower Danube, on both sides of the vast arc-shaped sweep of the Carpathian mountains, lies the territory of the Socialist Republic of Romania (the R.S.R., or Republica Socialistâ România) with an area of 237,500 square kilometres and a population of 19·1 million (1966 census). To the north and east this borders on Soviet territory–the Ukrainian Soviet Socialist Republic (including northern Bukovina) and the Soviet Socialist Republic of Moldavia–and in northern Dobrudja, between the bend in the Danube and the Black Sea, it shares one of the mouths of that great river that flows through the central Balkans.

Map 1. The Balkans today

The origins of these four countries and the establishment of their frontiers do not go far back in time. The latter was only completed after the second world war. For the previous five hundred years there had been a period of empire building characterized by the extension of power of the Ottoman empire across the Danube. Twice, in 1529 and 1683, its advance had been halted before Vienna by the united efforts of the peoples of central Europe. And after that, the Habsburgs and the sultan of Turkey shared possession of the Balkan peninsula with frontiers that changed from time to time. It was not until the internal disintegration of the empire that the basis was formed for a totally new political order in south-eastern Europe. The slow and steady retreat of Turkish power under pressure, which in diplomatic history is referred to as the 'eastern question', was hastened by uprisings during the nineteenth century of each of the Balkan countries against oppression and domination. Under the influence of the German Romantics, the French Revolution, and the west European concept of the state, the Christian peoples of the Balkans had unreservedly accepted the idea of the nation as a political unit in their struggle for freedom. It was inevitable that subsequent efforts to put these ideas into practice in a multi-national area where people were used to very different traditions should have had disastrous consequences. Clearly defined boundaries were completely alien to the various nationalities and minorities who lived there side by side with their many ethnic, religious, economic and social differences; and only reluctantly had they accepted the idea of a state with overall authority. It was not possible for them to realize the dream of creating a single empire based on national groups at the expense of their immediate neighbours without poisoning the atmosphere of their mutual relationships. The result in previous centuries had been that the somewhat haphazard frontier arrangements of the region had been continually thrown into question and endangered by irredentist movements.

The states that succeeded the Ottoman empire and the Austro-Hungarian monarchy enjoyed constitutional independence for but a comparatively short period during which they had to prove themselves able to deal with problems that other European nations had been facing throughout a whole century of steady development in far more favourable conditions. The Balkan countries shared the legacy of a past that was both colourful and unhappy, and that even the levelling processes of the post-war years could not altogether eradicate. This past was not to be forgotten after the artificial creation of the new states, whose internal politics were bedevilled by problems of integration of many kinds.

The strongly fissiparous tendencies that have survived to the present day were enhanced by the peculiar geographical characteristics of the Balkans. The varied land formation of the central area, stretching from one sea to another–the Adriatic in the west, and the Black Sea together with the Aegean in the east and south-east–and from the Danube-Sava axis in the north to the frontier of Greece in the south, has always had a powerful centrifugal influence, and has made any attempts to form bigger units difficult. The geography of south-eastern Europe lacks any obvious centre of gravity. The narrow Istrian-Dalmatian coast-line with its many bays facing groups of inhabited islands has held out great possibilities. But it is in fact separated from its natural hinterland by an almost impassable mountain ridge that forces the inhabitants of the coast-line to look towards the open seas, and brings them into contact with outside influences. The coastal cities were not only flourishing trade centres but also the gateways for foreign cultural influences–Roman, Byzantine, Venetian and Italian; and these have all left their marks on every branch of life in the region and have bestowed on the cities the characteristics that still delight the visitor today.

The upper regions of the western Balkan mountain range, rising behind the narrow coast-line, have given a special political and social character to the life of the peoples there. The natural barrier formed by the Dinaric mountains stretches in parallel ridges from the spur of the eastern Alps–the Carnic and Julian Alps, and the Karawanke mountains–in the north-west to the north Albanian mountains or the Prokletje in the south-east, and includes a large part of Slavonia, Upper Croatia (the Velebit and Kapela mountains), Bosnia (the Dinaric Alps) and Herzegovina as well as the former Serbian regions inland round the rivers Piva, Tara and Lim (the Raška (Rascia) and the Stari Vlach), and Montenegro and Albania. After bending slightly near Scutari, the range joins up with the Pindus mountains of northern Greece and Epirus, that is, western Macedonia and upper Albania, while to the north-east rises the Šar Planina. All these ranges form a chain that continues across the western part of Greece to the island of Crete. In the central Balkans the country is characterized by complete barrenness as it slopes abruptly towards the Adriatic coast, to which only a few of the larger rivers like the Zrmanja, Krka and Cetina are able to penetrate. Rarely are the river basins wide enough to provide means of communication with the interior.

In such remote mountain regions and valleys of the western Balkans, far away from the main lines of communication, ancient Balkan traditions and ways of life have to some extent survived into the twentieth century. These typical unchanging areas have had a strong influence in Balkan history. It is no accident that the mountain region was the cradle of the medieval Serbian state before it stretched down to the Adriatic coast and in a mighty movement of colonial expansion linked up with the lowlands of the Danube-Sava and Morava basins, and that the Montenegrin and Albanian mountain population only nominally submitted to Ottoman rule. Right into modern times the aristocratic and pea-sant republics—the Paštrovići Brotherhood near Budva, Poljica in the Cetina valley (which survived until 1807), and the Uskok sea fortress, Senj, south of Fiume and Sušak—remained their own masters and in their protected positions defied the attacks of foreign powers in the Gulf of Kotor, in the Ravni Kotari and in Bukovica and the hinterland of Zadar (Zara).

The geographical features of the inland area based on the axis of the Morava and Vardar rivers, an important line of communica-tion, are very different. That area is bounded to the south by Macedonia, a hotly contested region during the wars of national independence, and to the north by the lowlands of the Sava, the large tributary of the Danube. The landscape loses some of its mountainous character and slopes down in gentle terraces towards the junctions of the rivers Kulpa, Una, Vrbas, Bosna and

Drina with the Sava in the north and north-east, and to the Morava-Vardar valley in the east. The Niš basin occupies a strategic position in this valley since it is on a corridor north-east to the lower Danube, south-east to the Maritsa valley in Bulgaria and the Aegean Sea, and west across the central Balkans along the western Morava valley to Kotor (Cattaro), Dubrovnik (Ragusa) and the Adriatic. It has maintained its singular strategic and commercial importance as the junction of the most important roads of the area since the Middle Ages.

In the eastern section of the Balkans, communications are much easier. Here there exist continuous links in a west-east direction along the rivers Danube and Maritsa and along the ranges of mountains – the original Balkans, i.e. the Stara Planina or the Haemus mountains of antiquity, and the Rhodope chain to the south leading to the Aegean. The areas between the lower course of the Danube and the Balkan mountains (consisting of northern Bulgaria and the Dobrudja), and along the Maritsa (Thrace), are considered to be some of the most fertile in the Balkans.

The adjoining area to the north, the territory of the state of Romania, is dominated by the Carpathians (the east, south and western Carpathians), which stretch in a semi-circle round the plateau of Transylvania, separating the mountainous regions of the north-west from the river-crossed plains of the south and east – the plains of Wallachia and Moldavia.

In the history of south-eastern Europe there do not appear ever to have been strong impulses from within for political unification. On the contrary, the physically wide-open frontier to the north, the Pannonian region, and the long stretch of coastline have always attracted explorers and invaders. Because of its situation between two continents, the Balkan peninsula has been subject to the most varied outside influences over the centuries. It is the classic transit area – a meeting place for peoples and cultures where the western, oriental and Asiatic worlds, and central European and Mediterranean peoples, have all intermingled.

Many races of diverse origins have left indelible marks: the Celts, Romans, Teutons, Slavs, Hungarians, Greeks (especially the Byzantines), Italians, Turks, Normans, Franks and Germans, as

Map 2. The Balkans: physical features

well as the warring hordes of mounted nomads from central Asia. The latter penetrated again and again into the Balkans as they pushed forward along the migration routes across the steppes south of the Urals, and along the northern edge of the Black Sea. Some of them, like for instance the Hungarians (the Magyars) and the original Bulgars, took permanent root and established themselves among the European peoples.

The foreign conquerors and invaders advanced by the system of long-distance roads that stretches throughout south-eastern Europe. This system, determined by the physical lay-out of the area, threw the Balkans open to the outside world. Even today, international traffic such as the Orient-Express uses it, and internal commercial and cultural exchanges are carried out along a network of trunk roads.

The enormous importance of the Danube as a line of communication was recognized in ancient times. The methodical construction of garrison towns and the building of the road system had the purpose of safeguarding Roman domination, and above all protecting access to the important Balkan mountain passes. In the south the famous Roman road, the Via Egnatia, established the link between the old and the new Rome: opposite Brundisium (Brindisi) it led by way of Dyrrhachium (Durazzo or Durrës) through the Shkumbi valley to Lychnidos (Ohrid), Monastir (Bitolj), Salonica and Kavalla, and thence to Byzantium (Constantinople). Over the last stretch, the link road further north running diagonally across country from Styria to Constantinople attracted the main traffic. Roman travel records contain extensive descriptions of this second, long 'military road to Constantinople'. It went from Poetovio (Ptuj or Pettau) on the river Drava through Sirmium (Syrmia-Mitrowitz or Sremska Mitrovica) on the Sava, to Singidunum (Belgrade) on the Danube and Viminacium (Kostolac) near the Morava confluence; then to Naissus (Niš) and Serdica (Sofia), and from there over the Succi pass, the so-called 'Iron Gates', down to the Maritsa valley and via Philippopolis (Plovdiv) and Adrianople (Edirne) to Constantinople. This Byzantine 'royal route', which Slav, i.e. Serbian, records refer to as 'crski drum', was used by the Crusaders on their way to the Holy Land. Along it, too, the sultan of Turkey led his troops against Vienna. Part of it, the section between the Danube and Niš, runs parallel to the important north-south road along the Morava and Vardar valleys, the shortest route connecting the Danube basin with the Aegean. The course of that road is: Kostolac-Niš-Skopje-Salonica. Niš is also the meeting point for the two most important roads crossing the otherwise trackless western Balkans: the caravan route of the merchants of Ragusa and Cattaro—i.e., Dubrovnik and Kotor— which leads through the Neretva valley into inner Bosnia and Sarajevo, with connecting roads to Niš by way of the valley of the western Morava, and to the river Sava by the Bosna valley (today a railway route: Brod-Sarajevo-Mostar-Dubrovnik) and the Drina valley; and the more southern route, the Zeta route up the Drin valley to Prizren and Metohija, then over several passes to the Kosovo basin and Priština, and through the Toplica valley into the Niš basin. The development of these natural routes has much influenced the life of the Balkan peoples. It has meant considerable commercial and cultural exchange in the areas near and along-side them; but at the same time it has involved a continuous threat to the countryside, which through them was vulnerable to invaders and conquerors. The less accessible parts not suitable for road construction were territories where armies could retreat and con-solidate their defences.

In the *Géographie Humaine* of Jovan Cvijić and the folklore research of such figures as Gesemann, Gavazzi, Matl and A. Schmaus, with their particular views of cultures, a distinction is made between the characteristics of the different cultural areas. There is a distinct area of Balkan-Byzantine culture with a strong Oriental element in the continental and east Balkan regions that are now opened up to trade—the world of the Balkan middle-class citizen and the typical Turkish country town. Then next to this, in the upper regions of the western Balkans, is an area typified by a patriarchal way of life, with people of pronounced physical and social features who believe in the heroic male as an ideal. Here the most favourable conditions have prevailed for keeping alive archaic national characteristics. In the west, along the coast, lies a zone with an Italo-Slav Adriatic culture. While in the north, the central

European cultural zone or Pannonia (that is, north-east Slovenia, north Croatia, Slavonia, Srem, Vojvodina (Baranja, Bačka and Banat)) connects the Balkan peninsula with the European continent. The reason this complex environment has made its impact so firmly on its temporary inhabitants is that, in spite of ethnic, cultural and religious differences, a common and lasting Balkan cultural synthesis has developed. But the national and racial frontiers do not coincide with the cultural ones.

The confusing ethnic structure of south-eastern Europe is the end-product of centuries of continuous assimilation of local and foreign elements. Not only have different ethnic groups lived side by side, but also an intermingling of characteristics has frequently taken place. As a result of the far-reaching processes of social reconstruction of the last two centuries, ethnic changes have been brought about in the closed social structure through the movement of people from lower social strata. They have narrowed the gulf between the political and intellectual ruling classes and the lower classes.

The original population of the peninsula before it was overrun by the Indo-European races has left few visible traces. Lepensky Vir, a village site on the Danube in Yugoslavia dating back to about 5000 B.C., is exceptional. The controversy among philologists as to whether there are pre-Indo-European linguistic substrata in the Mediterranean area and the Balkans—one aspect of which is the so-called 'Pelasgian' problem in Greece—seems now to have been resolved. For it has been established that a number of root words in the southern part of the Balkans which can be traced to the period before the historically recorded immigrations of Indo-European peoples, the Greeks, Thracians, Illyrians, Macedonians and others, have their origin in the 'Indo-European language'. Even so, there are strong arguments for not excluding the possibility of an earlier pre-Indo-European linguistic substratum.

Opinions are divided about how far the pre-Greek Indo-European languages of the 'satem' group really spread to the north. There are not many traces of them in the language maps of south-eastern Europe, partly owing to the emigration of a number of races–like the Phrygians and the speakers of Asiatic languages such as Lycian, Lydian, Carian, Pamphylian–and above all to the profound effect of Greek, Roman and Slav influences on this cultural melting-pot. That also applies to the pre-Roman population of the inner regions of the Balkans, the Illyrian peoples in the west and the Thracians in the east, who followed the waves of Greek immigration from the north in the second millennium and subjugated the original populations in those areas. The words of their languages which survived were absorbed in the general process of integration that took place in subsequent centuries, and have only left traces among the mysterious people of Albania, though elements of their culture survive in the popular beliefs, folklore and peasant culture of the Balkan races. In this connection it is interesting to note that the names of the larger rivers have links with the early period before the arrival of the Romans and Slavs, e.g. the Danube, Sava, Drava, Mura, Tisza, Kulpa, Una, Vrbas, Bosna, Drina, Neretva, Zeta, Ibar, Morava, Iskŭr and Maritsa.

From about 500 B.C. onwards, first the Greeks and then the Romans completely transformed the Balkans. The Greek influence began with the numerous trading settlements created during the second important period of colonization that took place in the sixth century B.C. along the coastlines of the Black Sea, the Aegean, the Ionian Sea and the Adriatic. Although colonization by the Greeks was confined to the coastal areas, the Greek way of life penetrated deep into the country in the wake of commercial exchanges with the 'barbarian' hinterland, and produced a special mixture of Hellenic and barbarian cultures.

The Roman influence, on the other hand, originated in the camps of the legions and garrison towns in Macedonia, along the Dalmatian-Albanian coast and in the Danube region. Challenged by Illyrian buccaneers in the third century B.C., the Romans decided to overrun the Balkan peninsula and gain political ascendancy. In their efforts to keep Macedonia's dangerous lust for power in check, they were then drawn further and further into the interior. After the establishment of a centralized administration based on the Roman provincial system, and bitter minor wars

23

which finally ended in peace in the interior, the local people had to change their way of life totally and accept the superiority of the culture and language of the Roman empire. Provincial Latin became their everyday language and the other languages slowly died out. But all-powerful Rome had to share its authority in the Balkans with the superior culture of the Greeks. South-eastern Europe became bilingual. A distinct linguistic and cultural division can in fact be traced from west to east straight across the peninsula along a line from Durazzo (Dyrrhachium) through the Drin valley to Skopje, and along the uplands of the Balkan ranges to the east. Inscriptions preserved on tombstones have made it possible to reconstruct the dividing line. In the area to the south of it where Greek was the everyday spoken language, i.e. in Macedonia, southern Albania and Bulgaria, Latin was not more than the official language of the empire for a few centuries more.

The stormy period of the Germanic migrations when the western and eastern Goths, that is, the Visigoths and Ostrogoths, passed through the Balkans left almost no trace, in contrast with that of the Slav population movements which after the sixth century A.D. brought about profound changes in the map of south-eastern Europe. At the time of the greatest movement of Slav settlers between A.D. 600 and A.D. 800, most of the inland region was occupied by Slav peasants, and even a central area like the Peloponnese was threatened with occupation by settlers. The original inhabitants – the Greeks in the south and the Latin-speaking provincial populations in the north – were squeezed back to the coast, the islands, and the mountain regions, though some of them were able to take refuge in fortified towns. The whole inland area was lost to the Byzantine empire through the pressure of this slow migration. The few remaining coastal stretches, islands and places of retreat in its hands were completely cut off from the interior, and owing to the withdrawal of the land forces could only be held through the efforts of the imperial fleet.

The Roman inhabitants of the provinces of Dalmatia who withdrew to the coastal towns managed to hold their own against the Slav settlers and preserve their identity. It was not until a later period that these towns came under Slav influence. Still more interesting is the fate of those settlers in the Roman provinces who retreated up into the mountains. As the new Slav immigrants cultivated the better land, they forced the local inhabitants into the barren highlands where they reverted to the primitive life of shepherds and nomads. Traces of this process, a step backwards in economic and cultural development, can still be discerned in the words of Slav origin in the Albanian and Romanian languages. Although the Slav races succeeded in establishing themselves as the dominant ethnic element in the central Balkans, strong racial minorities continued to exist and made their influence felt in the border areas and mountain regions. The Slav rulers themselves invited many foreigners to work in the mines, especially in the Bosnian and Serbian districts, with offers of privileges; and the mining industry provided the economic basis for the development of the Balkan countries in the Middle Ages. German miners from Hungary, referred to as 'Sachsens' or 'Sasi' by the Slavs, together with prosperous merchants and mine-owners from the Adriatic coastal towns, gave the fast developing mining settlements, and Ragusa in particular, a pronounced 'Latin' character.

In the Balkans, towns, in the strict sense of the word, remained alien social structures well into the nineteenth century. In the Danubian area they were predominantly German and on the Adriatic coast largely Venetian in character; while in the central area their development was based on late Byzantine or Turkish-cum-oriental foundations. The rise of Ottoman power after the end of the fourteenth century accelerated this development. Trade and the crafts were largely closed to the native population and were almost exclusively in the hands of Turks, Greeks, Armenians and Jews, who settled in separate districts according to race.

This state of affairs had many repercussions in the social history of the existing rural population. A rise in social status in the towns involved a diminution in national character. The emancipation of the Balkan states in the nineteenth and twentieth centuries had therefore not merely to contend with foreign political domination – that of Turkey and Austria-Hungary – but also with overwhelming foreign influences in social and intellectual life. Years of accumulated bitterness led to repeated outbreaks of violence: it gave vent to the latent resentment against Greeks, Hungarians and above all Jews. The expulsion of the Germans from the area in our time is only the last phase in a long process.

The continuous movement of populations has been an essential part of Balkan history. Such movements continued throughout the centuries of Ottoman domination. The Turkish element in south-eastern Europe was not simply represented by an upper class of Ottoman officials. Turkish peasants from Anatolia also settled in small groups, though only eastern Thrace – the region immediately around the capital, Istanbul, and Edirne (Adrianople) – finally became a purely Turkish settlement. But the growing number of settlements of Albanian mountain races, or Arnauts, that came increasingly under Turkish influence, had more important consequences for the ethnological map of the Balkans. These settlements stretched across western Macedonia and the original Serbian regions (i.e. Raška) and reached into Bulgaria, the Peloponnese and the Greek islands. Moreover, the foreign domination of the Ottoman empire triggered off even before the end of the fourteenth century the great migration of the Serbs to the north, with its lasting effects. It eventually encompassed the south Hungarian territory across the Danube where the so-called 'Raitza' cities were created.

That fact was to be of great importance during the national awakening of the Serbs. With the slow advance of the Habsburgs, those Serbs who had settled in southern Hungary early on became incorporated into a highly developed political system. As a result, they were in a better position to bring into being the intellectual class from which famous national heroes such as Dositej Obradović emerged. The 'military frontier' deliberately established by the Habsburgs against the Turks from the Adriatic coast across through Croatia, Slavonia, Srem and Banat to Transylvania had the same kind of effect in rousing national consciousness by the settlement of Balkan refugees as did the emigration of freedom-loving individuals into the inaccessible inland mountain regions of Montenegro, Albania and the Balkan range.

This picture of the ethnic structure of the Balkans is further confused by the existence of different religions and denominations. Contemporary statistics show that in addition to the dominating influence of the Catholic Church in the north-west, in the northern Adriatic area, Slavonia, Croatia and north Albania, and that of the Orthodox church in the south and south-west, there exist considerable Muslim minorities in Bosnia, central and southern Albania and west Macedonia, as well as the remnants of a Jewish community.

The division of ecclesiastical jurisdiction in the Balkans between the eastern and western churches is the result of a long-drawn-out process. Confronted with the rival missionary efforts of the religious centres of Rome and Constantinople, the Serbs were the last to adopt an unequivocal position. It was not until the establishment of a Serbian national church under St. Sava, supported by the Greek patriarch, at the beginning of the thirteenth century that the Serbs finally rejected Rome. The drawing of political frontiers in later years preserved and even sharpened the denominational differences.

Despite the predominant political position of Islam, it was in Albania and Bosnia alone that it succeeded in penetrating the spheres of spiritual influence of the Christian churches. The explanation is to be found in certain peculiar characteristics of Islamic law, which, if only for fiscal reasons, did not accept the idea of subjecting a conquered population to missionaries. In most cases mass conversions among the Christian population were motivated by economic rather than idealistic considerations. Whereas the Serbian and Bulgarian Orthodox aristocracy was largely levelled down and in some cases physically eliminated under Turkish rule, the Bosnian upper class, which accepted the Islamic faith, managed to survive and keep its leading social position. A century of anti-ecclesiastical and anti-clerical movements in the shape of Bogomilism had prepared the ground for a religious decline. In Albania the justifiable fear of severe Turkish reprisals provided the impetus in the seventeenth century for religious conversions. Historical records of the widespread crypto-Christianity in the areas dominated by the Islamic faith throw a revealing light on the true motives behind such proceedings.

Religious divisions and differences undoubtedly had lasting effects on the cultural make-up of each of the Balkan countries.

Opposition between the Catholic Croats and the Orthodox Serbs, and between the Catholics of north Albania and the Muslims of central and southern Albania, is partly explicable in terms of differences in religious outlook. Differences and different nuances in the Catholic and Orthodox interpretations of the Christian faith–for instance, in their concepts of the world, their scale of values as regards the subjugation of human beings, the question of political and social conduct, and their fundamental attitudes towards the power of the state–have led to markedly different developments. Even today these are in evidence to a greater or lesser degree in the secular and spiritual life of the Balkan peoples. The use of Cyrillic or Latin characters according to one's ecclesiastical allegiance is the most obvious example.

Such religious divisions did not actually become cultural divisions in the real sense. This was because they were limited to the most cultured sections of society. The culture of the ordinary people and the life of the lower classes were governed by different laws. These can be seen in various manifestations. Unaffected by differences of creed, they brought about a common 'Balkan' social structure with its own customs, folklore and way of life.

More central than the religious divisions were various political, economic and social factors. In the later period of development, the desire for a separate state based on nationality was stronger than religious loyalties, and–mainly among the Serbs, Bulgarians, Romanians and Greeks–repeatedly prevented the rise of the consciousness of belonging to a community based on the Orthodox faith. Throughout the period of Turkish rule and of national rebirth, nationalism and religion were closely allied. There was a direct interplay between the forces working for political independence and those working for religious autonomy, and the achievement of the former was invariably followed by the latter. The concern of the church over the political destiny of its faithful increased with the special conditions prevailing under Turkish rule. Leaders of the church emerged among spokesmen for the sultan's Christian subjects who were recognized by him as having a definite political mandate. Orthodox monasteries in Serbia and Bulgaria proved themselves the true upholders of national traditions as well as places of refuge for those fighting for freedom, and thus won the respect of the ordinary man. The church's political involvement continued into the era of national renaissance. In Montenegro, it was the bishops of Cetinje who challenged the ruling dynasty and led their people to political independence. Thus, because of the unusual external circumstances in south-eastern Europe, the urge to establish national churches which would make Christian teaching a reality, and the bitter rejection of continued efforts under the Turks to hellenize the Orthodox faith were more fundamental characteristics of the period than attempts to unify the Orthodox church, and common resistance to outside attack.

Their special geographical conditions and constantly changing historical evolution made it impossible for the Balkan countries to emerge as a unity. The Balkan peninsula, a typical transit area, as we have said, only favoured the loosest kind of political organization for its inhabitants. It never proved feasible to establish a firm political structure that could control all the border areas. The motley collection of peoples who settled and mixed with each other there was more open to external influences so that their development was intimately connected with the history of neighbouring nations. This factor is still of vital importance for a full comprehension of the history of the region. It is often overlooked in histories that are written from a narrow, nationalistic point of view and that trace the rise of the modern nation state from origins in the distant past. The history of the whole area can only be understood from a universal standpoint. One must be prepared to look beyond the framework of nationality and be able to relate the individual fortunes of the south-eastern European nations to the history of central Europe, the Mediterranean and the Near East.

Because of their particular ethnic structure, the Balkan lands have not merely played a part in the historical evolution of their neighbours. They have always been drawn into and affected by the game of power politics played by the great powers as well. In their drive for territorial expansion, powerful countries nearby have intervened with force time and again to prevent the formation of larger independent units, and have subjected the local populations to foreign régimes. It is in this way that political separatism, encouraged by the physical features of the region and by strong external influences, has become the special characteristic of Balkan history.

2

RACIAL SEPARATISM AND
ROMAN IMPERIALISM

The centuries preceding Roman rule witnessed the formation of ephemeral governments of a supra-regional character among the indigenous racial groupings of south-eastern Europe, but they never saw the establishment of any lasting forms of political organization. Herodotus, who lived from *c*. 485 to 425 B.C. and was a shrewd observer, was already aware of the lack of will for unity among the Thracian races in the east of the Balkans when he wrote his important work on Greek history. It contains a number of interesting ethnographical digressions.

'The Thracians are, after the Indians, the most numerous of all peoples. And if they had a leader, or were truly united, they could be unconquerable and by far the most powerful of all peoples. That is my opinion. But since it is in no way possible that this could ever come about, they are correspondingly weak.'

Historiae V, 3

The flourishing Odrysian empire of the fifth and fourth centuries B.C., which reached its zenith under king Seuthes I (424–410), temporarily freed the Thracians from Persian influence and led them towards unity. However, it collapsed even before the days of Macedonian supremacy brought about by Philip II (359–336) in the Thracian wars of 358 to 341. Racial separatism proved too strong, and it also imposed its way of life very quickly on foreign invaders. The Macedonian conquerors themselves were unable to find any lasting basis for a stable political structure in the Thracian region. Philip II and his son Alexander the Great (336–323 B.C.), the two outstanding personalities and leaders of the fourth century, did finally force the Thracians to submit to their

31

sovereignty after bitter battles involving severe loss of life. Immediate neighbours, too, such as the Illyrian peoples in the west and
the Scythians living in the northern hinterland above the Black
Sea, were also unable to put up effective resistance to the aggres-
siveness of the invading Macedonians, who under Alexander
created a world empire in the space of a few years. And out of this
shortlived bout of imperialism there was to emerge a unified
structure under the Antigonid dynasty that included Greece and
the greater part of the Balkan peninsula as well.

But it only survived on the fringe of the ancient world in the
large cities of the eastern Mediterranean, and it crumbled during
the Diadochean wars of the third century over the succession to
Alexander's empire. Thus, though the dangerous thrust of the
Celts (the 'Galatians' of St. Paul's *Epistles*) into Thrace and
Macedonia in 281–280 was halted by Antigonus Gonatas at the
battle of Lysimacheia in 277, Celts were able to dominate the local
peoples of Thracian origin around Tylis (Tulovo) in the Balkan
mountains up to 212 B.C. If the Macedonian empire which outlived the death of Alexander, did much to promote Hellenic
culture among the races living in the east of the Balkans, it was
nevertheless a mere episode in their political development.

The efforts of the Macedonians to bring about unity were
in time completely shattered by the onslaught of Roman legions
coming from the west and thrusting into the Balkan interior. From
the beginning of the third century B.C., the Macedonian empire
had suffered defeats at the hands of the Romans, and as early as
197 B.C. king Philip V (221–179), who had formed an alliance with
Hannibal against the Romans, had suffered a crushing defeat at
Cynoscephalae in Thessaly. His son Perseus (179–168) eventually
succumbed to the armies of L. Aemilius Paulus at the battle of
Pydna in 168.

In the period that followed the establishment of the Roman
system of provincial administration, the province of Macedonia
was created in 148 B.C., and it played an important role in the
pacification of the peoples of the inner Balkans. The Bessi, the
Maidi and the Triballi were in continuous rebellion, and the rebels
were encouraged by the Pontine king Mithridates VI Eupator

1	Olbia	9	Brundisium	17	Byzantium	25	Syracusae	33 Cyzikos
2	Tyrus	10	Heraclea	18	Chalcedon	26	Delphi	34 Pergamum
3	Chersonesos	11	Tarentum	19	Amastris	27	Athens	35 Magnesia
4	Callatis	12	Apollonia	20	Heraclea	28	Corinthos	36 Sardes
5	Roma	13	Pella	21	Panormus	29	Sparta	37 Ephesus
6	Neapolis	14	Thessalonica	22	Agrigentum	30	Illion	
7	Beneventum	15	Philippi	23	Gela	31	Abydos	
8	Ausculum	16	Lysimacheia	24	Rhegium	32	Ankyra	

Map 3. Greece, Rome and the Balkan area, third century B.C.

(120–63 B.C.). It took several campaigns–the so-called Mithridatic Wars–to defeat both him and the great Dacian empire which had grown up in the Carpathian and Danubian areas around 60 B.C. under Burebista. The latter was in the end the victim of a conspiracy in 45 or 44 B.C.

It was only after long hesitation that the Roman imperial power decided to intervene on a permanent basis in the Balkans, and lend an ear to the entreaties for help from the Greek coastal towns and Italian merchants. The reason for these appeals was not so much the rise of a south Illyrian empire under king Agron (c. 250–230 B.C.) and his wife Teuta (230–228) around Scutari and the Bay of Cattaro–the empire of the Ardiaei–as the growing threat to navigation in the Adriatic from Illyrian pirates, as we saw in chapter I. There were also other strategic considerations. For a whole century the Roman empire had been involved in a running fight with the Illyrian and Celtic races along the Adriatic coast. The turning point at last came when, in the course of their Illyrian campaigns, Octavian and Agrippa methodically advanced into the interior against the rebellious Iapudes, Pannonians and Dalmatians (35–33 B.C.), and annexed the western Balkans right up to the Pannonian plain. The Danube became the frontier of the Roman empire, the province of Pannonia being created in 33 B.C. After a dangerous rebellion in Illyria and Pannonia had been put down in A.D. 6, this frontier was finally secured by Tiberius in his military campaigns of A.D. 8–9.

Further to the east, the governor of Macedonia, M. Licinius Crassus, had succeeded in suppressing the last attempts at rebellion on the part of the local tribes in 29–18 B.C. in his campaigns against the Bastarnae, Daci and Getae. In either A.D. 46 or 44 the provinces of Moesia and Thrace were created here. As master of the Balkan peninsula, Rome could now go forward with the establishment of a new political order.

The completion of the carefully planned network of Roman roads mentioned earlier, the building of fortresses, and the creation for the first time of an effective system of government in the provinces, established a lasting foundation for the unification of south-eastern Europe. We owe the detailed description of this

Roman road system to a number of road maps from the later period of the Roman empire, the *Tabula Peutingeriana* from the third century, and the *Itinerarium Antonini Augusti* and *Itinerarium Hierosolymitanum* or *Burdigalense* of the fourth century. There are also lists of *mansiones* (overnight quarters), *mutationes* (stations for changing horses), *castella*, *praesidia*, and *turres* (strongholds and fortifications). In addition to the famous Via Egnatia which had been built to guarantee the security of Macedonia, the main road from Belgrade across the eastern Balkans became increasingly important, as I have said. Like so many other monuments constructed in the Roman period, it is associated with the name of the emperor Trajan (98–117), still a living force in many local traditions as one of the greatest organizers of Roman rule in the Balkans. After the conquest of the Dacians and their warrior-king Decebalus, he safeguarded the defence of the Roman empire in the north for a century and a half, from 107 to 271, by annexing the province of Dacia Trajana in A.D. 107 in present-day Transylvania. It was the policy of the Roman empire to protect its Balkan and other possessions from the attacks of barbarians by an expensive defence system along the northern frontier, the Danube-Rhine *limes*. For the next two centuries the Balkan peoples, united under the *imperium Romanum*, enjoyed unprecedented economic and cultural prosperity and, serving in the Roman army, they made a substantial contribution to the security of the Roman empire. The rise of the so-called Illyrian emperors in the third century was achieved by contingents that were largely recruited from the indigenous population. The Balkan provinces provided a number of the most capable emperors and army leaders, men that were remarkably skilful in identifying their loyalty to the empire with their local provincial interests. The emperor Aurelian (270–275), for example, was born in Moesia; Diocletian (284–305), the great reorganizer of the empire, was of Dalmatian origin; his opponent Galerius came from the country near Sofia; and later on, Justin (518–527), who rose to the highest honours in the empire after following an officer's career in the imperial army, was of Macedonian peasant origin. His nephew and successor, Justinian I (527–565), was born in the neighbourhood of Skopje.

The Roman civil service gave opportunities to many local families to gain important governmental and administrative posts, and this trend went even further as the empire's centre of gravity gradually moved from the Italian provinces to the danger points on its periphery–above all in the Danubian provinces and on the eastern frontier of Asia Minor. In face of increasing external threats, the emperors often had to transfer their residence from Rome to their army headquarters in the field. This had important constitutional consequences, for the election of the emperors came to depend increasingly on the vote of the army and the officers' corps rather than that of the senatorial class which had till then had the decisive vote. Moreover, the frequent presence of the imperial court in Balkan garrison towns and army camps much enhanced the importance of the Balkan provinces and implanted the idea of moving the centre of the empire east.

This was the motive for the founding of Constantinople in the year A.D. 330–an event which was to have the most far-reaching consequences. After the division of the empire in A.D. 395, Roman defence in the Balkans was continued from Constantinople as the central point of the eastern empire. That defence remained a permanent feature of Roman and Byzantine foreign policy. The devastating invasions by successive waves of 'barbarians' in later times and the formation of various governments by the invading races were looked on by the Byzantine emperors from a single viewpoint: their aim became the preservation of the existing territorial boundaries by a series of fictitious legal enactments.

For a thousand years, the history of the peninsula was typified on the one hand by the annexation of land and such formations of governments by the barbarians, and on the other by defence measures and attempts to reconquer these territories by the Roman and Byzantine emperors. In the time of the 'Roman' emperors, the imperial frontier along the Danube had to be held against massive pressure from the Germanic races. By well planned military operations into the hinterland and across the Danube, and also by diplomacy–e.g. the creation of a series of vassal states behind the frontier line of the Danube–the threats of invasion were overcome. The Marcomanni war of 166 to 180 had ended in a Roman victory under Marcus Aurelius (161–180). But only a hundred years later, in 271, the emperor Aurelian, under pressure from the Goths, was forced to evacuate Dacia, the Roman outpost in the area beyond the Danube.

The continuous movement of nomadic peoples in the steppes of central Asia gave rise to progressively violent attacks on the frontiers of the empire along the lower Danube, which at last collapsed. The first invasion of consequence was made by the western Goths or Visigoths. Fleeing from the advancing Huns, they forced their way into imperial territory, and in the bloody battle of Adrianople in 378 won a victory over the emperor Valens. In 382, Theodosius I was forced to allow the western Goths to live on imperial territory and establish themselves with full legal rights. It was the first time this had happened in the history of the empire.

The interior of the Balkan peninsula passed through a turbulent period of transition after the Germanic migrations, which were accompanied by devastation, plunder and destruction. The chief migration was that of the western Goths under Alaric. They had even forced a temporary entry into Rome in 410 and succeeded in imposing their influence on imperial policy. The Goth Gainas, the *magister militum praesentalis* (commander-in-chief of the palace troops), and Alaric Aspar, who married a daughter of emperor Leo I and rose temporarily to the rank of Caesar, and his sons Ardabur and Patricius were impressive examples of the predominant Germanic influence at the imperial court in Constantinople during the fifth century. The forcible removal of Aspar and the departure of the eastern Goths or Ostrogoths under Theodoric in 488 freed the eastern half of the empire from the Germanic peril at the expense of the western half, which fell to them in turn. The unity of the Roman empire thus broke down owing to events following the migrations. The division of the empire in 395, at first established for dynastic reasons, was to become irrevocable.

The frontier between its two halves now ran across the western part of the Balkan peninsula. However, with the invasions of the barbarians later on, it was gradually pushed back further and further towards the west. Illyria in the time of Constantine (324–337) had comprised, as part of the prefecture of Italy, the

RAETIA

Lauriacum

Iuvavum (Salzburg)

Vindobona (Vienna)

NORICUM

Savaria

Aquincum

Teurnia

Virunum

PANNONIA

superior

TRANSPADANA

VENETIA

Aquileia

Verona

Patavium (Padua)

Savus

LIGURIA

Padus

Parentium

Siscia

inferior

AEMILIA

Bononia

Pola

Mursa

Ravenna

Sirmium

Ariminum

Ilyricum

UMBRIA

Burnum

Arretium

ETRURIA

Perusia

Salonae

DALMATIA

Falerio

Narona

PICENUM

CORSICA

Tiber

SAMNIUM

MARE ADRIATICUM

Doclea

Roma

LATIUM ET
CAMPANIA

Canusium

Barium

Dyrrhachium

Neapolis

Beneventum

Puteoli

APULIA

Brundisium

SARDINIA

Tarentum

Apollonia

Byllis

Paestum

EPIRUS

Buthrotum

LUCANIA ET
BRUTTIUM

Corcyra

SICILIA

MARE INTERNUM

Map 4. The Balkan area under the Roman empire, second century A.D.

dioceses of Pannonia, Dacia and Macedonia. At the division of the empire, the diocese of Pannonia had been the only one ceded to the western empire; Dacia and Macedonia were allotted to the east. The collapse of the western empire at the beginning of the fifth century had then brought the entire Adriatic coast under the sovereignty of an east Roman emperor. In the middle of the sixth century the emperor Justinian I, assisted by the great military achievements of his army commanders, Belisarius and Narses, succeeded in temporarily reuniting east and west. He destroyed the Ostrogothic empire in Italy. But his conquests on the Italian mainland soon began to slip from the grasp of the eastern Roman empire when in 568 the Lombards under their king Alboin marched out of the regions they had occupied in Pannonia. The exarch of Ravenna managed to stand out against the new Italian rulers until 751.

By his extravagant and wasteful policy of moving large contingents of troops to the Italian, North African, and near eastern battlefields, Justinian had deprived the Danubian frontier of the essential forces necessary for resisting threats of invasion from the north-east. His attempts at 'reconquest' caused a considerable weakening of the northern frontier, and indirectly encouraged the large-scale migrations of the Slavs, which were to alter the interior landscape of the Balkans so radically. These migrations were closely connected with large-scale shifts of population in the steppe regions to the north of the Black Sea.

It was not by accident that the defence of the Byzantine empire was confronted with new dangers from the steppes. For some time past, Greek diplomacy had been establishing links with the peoples north of the Caucasus and the Black Sea, and had been taking preventive measures from friendly observation posts in the Crimea. But diplomatic measures could only halt the pressure of the migratory peoples for a while. The Avars who had moved west were merely dissuaded from renewed attacks for a few years by the federal arrangements of 558, and by 561 they had appeared in the lower Danube region in search of land. When Justinian I and his successor Justinian II (565–578) stopped them from entering imperial territory, they and the Lombards turned against the

Gepids, and after destroying them in 567 took up residence in Dacia and the eastern half of Pannonia. With the departure of the Lombards in 568, they enlarged their sphere of influence towards the Alps in the west, and beyond the Carpathian basin to the north and north-east.

The Byzantine empire was unable to raise any substantial defence forces to counter the threat posed by this concentration of power in the Pannonian area, even after the renunciation of Justinian I's imperialistic policies. In spite of the loss of the strategically important Sirmium, which fell to the Avar Khan Bajan in 582 after a two-year siege, the brave emperor Maurice (582–602) and his commander-in-chief Priscus did succeed in holding the Danube boundary for a time; but then an army rebellion wiped out all earlier successes. The incompetence of the soldier-emperor Phocas (602–610) accelerated the catastrophe. The rising Avar-Slav tide steadily flooded the Balkans and as early as 626 they were besieging the capital of the empire, Constantinople.

For nearly two centuries, south-eastern Europe was to be withdrawn from the area of Byzantine rule, and the changes that took place in the inland population structure during the period were mostly irreversible by the time the Byzantine counter-offensive began in about 800. The appropriation of land by Slav peasants could no longer be nullified. Its consequences have influenced the fate of the Balkans right up to the present time.

3

LAND APPROPRIATION BY THE SLAVS AND THE FIRST EFFORTS AT EMPIRE BUILDING

Contemporary sources are silent about the details and circumstances of land appropriation by the Slavs. But after the beginning of the sixth century, and as early as the reign of Justin (518–527), references can be found to occasional invasions by 'Bulgarian', Slav and Antean hordes across the Danube frontier. The ethnic constitution of the 'Bulgars', who had already overrun Thrace towards the end of the fifth century, presents problems. In existing sources it is difficult to find any definite references to connections between them and the Ogur races (the Kutrigurs and Utigurs). However, we shall have something positive to say about the groups of Bulgars of Turkic origin who freed themselves from Avar domination in the area north of the Caucasus at the beginning of the seventh century and under Kovrat formed their own short-lived empire (see page 45): Byzantine records were to describe this as the 'ancient Great Bulgaria'. The Slavs and Antes who figure as the two main Slav racial groups in the sixth-century historical records of Jordanes, Procopius of Caesarea (c. 490–c. 562) and Pseudo-Mauricius were partly subject to the Avars. Already at the beginning of the fifth century they appear to have been gradually and peacefully extending their settlements from regions north of the Carpathians, some of them being caught up then in the westward movement of the Avars and arriving at the frontiers of the empire in the Danube region.

Justinian I had had to give way to the growing pressure of these peasant-farmers. He had decided to let individual groups of them settle on imperial territory, and play off the Antes and Bulgars against each other by diplomacy. But in spite of many minor successes in the defence of the empire in the first three decades of the sixth century, there had been no stemming the tide of invasion in the Danube region. Avar, Slav and Bulgar hordes had overrun the Balkan interior in extensive plundering campaigns and ventured as far as the gates of Salonica and Constantinople. Only the intervention of the Danube fleet had succeeded in postponing for a while the complete collapse of the Danube frontiers. The open country of the Balkan provinces fell defenceless to the invaders.

The penetration of Slav influence in the lowlands had actually begun at a time when the military balance had been uncertain. The simultaneous threat from Persia, which had been menacing the eastern frontier of the empire, had weakened the Byzantine defences at a crucial stage in their quarrel with the Avar Khan at the end of the sixth century. When the emperor Maurice, after a victorious campaign in the east, had finally been able to devote his attention to the Balkan problem with renewed energy, an army rebellion had quickly destroyed the fruits of his military success, as we saw in the previous chapter. In 602, both the Balkan and the eastern fronts collapsed. The demise of the empire seemed inevitable. But the situation was saved by the son of the exarch of Carthage, Heraclius, who took the rebellion in hand and put an end to the tyrannical rule of the emperor Phocas.

During his long reign lasting from 610 to 641, Heraclius not only succeeded in solving the Persian problem after several battles, which at last enabled him to forge ahead into the centre of the kingdom of the Sassanids, king Chosroes II being overthrown and his son surrendering; he also managed to bring some order into the chaotic conditions in the Balkans. He was helped by the enormous loss of prestige suffered by the Avars after their unsuccessful siege of Constantinople in 626. This had demolished their claims to power and had immensely encouraged their allies in their efforts to become independent. Byzantine diplomacy exploited the occasion and once more attempted to bring the inner Balkans under its control.

The Byzantine emperor had thus been able to exert an influence in the matter of land appropriation by the Slav races, and he had introduced new forms of subject relationship. The imperial author of the tenth century, Constantine VII Porphyrogenitus, to whom

Most of the Byzantine Territory north and west of the broken line
in the Balkans was lost to the invading tribes after the middle of
the 7th century.

Map 5. Slav and other invaders, sixth to eighth centuries

44

we are indebted for most detailed information about the Slav settlers in the Balkan provinces in his *De Administrando Imperio*, sees a direct connection between the arrival of 'Croats' and 'Serbs' and the politics of Heraclius. To help him keep the Avars in check, he is said to have invited the Slavs into Dalmatian territory and to have allotted them areas where they could settle.

The races collectively referred to as Croats and Serbs appear therefore to have arrived in the Balkans at the end of the period when Slavs were occupying the land, and at a moment when the collapse of the Avar empire had opened up access across the Danube. Already in 623 a Frankish merchant called Samo had taken advantage of the apparent weakness of the Avar Khan and established an independent state among the Slav races in Bohemian-Moravian territory, which, thanks to its commercially strategic position at the intersection of several important trade routes, managed to survive for several decades.

Another breakaway from Avar domination brought about in 635 by the Onogur Kovrat to the east—in the regions north of the Black Sea—was to have a profound effect on the destiny of the Balkan peoples. He became friendly with the emperor Heraclius and proved himself a true ally until his death in 642. But the 'Great Bulgaria' which he established did not survive for long. It broke up in the middle of the seventh century before the advance of the Chazars, pressing forward from the interior of Asia. One group of 'Bulgars' was to move northwards and form the kindgom of the Volga-Bulgars; and another group was to appear in 680 in the area of the lower Danube under the leadership of Kovrat's son, Asparuch (or Isperich), and force an entry into imperial territory. In accordance with the treaty of 681, the emperor Constantine IV (668–685) was compelled to recognize this empire of Bulgars of Turkic origin controlling the territory between the Balkan highlands and the Dniester from their capital, Pliska. The greater portion of the Slav races of the eastern Balkans were to be absorbed into this expanding Bulgar domain. It was when the original Bulgar[1] upper class intermarried with the mass of the Slav

[1] In English a distinction is made between 'Bulgar' and 'Bulgarian'. 'Bulgarian' = Bulgar + Slav. (Translator's note.)

population that the Slav race called the Bulgarians finally emerged. Byzantine records also give the names of many Slav tribes who settled as far south as the hinterland of Salonica, central Greece and even the Peloponnese.

The explanation for the success this mixture of Bulgar and Slav peoples had in building a vast empire probably lies in the special situation of the Slavs in the Balkans. The social and political structure of the immigrant Slav peoples is insufficiently known. Contemporary writers, however, all place great emphasis on their strongly individualistic way of life. Procopius in his historical work on the wars against the Persians, Vandals and Goths, to which he added ethnographical appendices, uses the term 'democracy' to characterize the system of rule of the Slovenes and Antes: '. . . they are not ruled by one man, but have lived from ancient times in a state of democracy. . . .' Blood and family relationships were still the dominant forces in any social arrangement.

Particular forms of domestic community surviving well into the nineteenth century such as the large family (the *zadruga*) in the Dinaric region of the western Balkans have been compared with those of the Slav races which developed from the special conditions of the migratory period. Larger territorial communities, the *župas* or districts, often emerged after unions of individual families ruled by patriarchal 'heads of the family' (the *domaćin* or *starešina*) had formed village settlements (the *bratstvo*, brotherhoods or tribes) with a common overlord (*čelnik*). The territorial units of a tribal area developed as a rule around a fortress (*grad*). However, strong racial separatism was an obstacle to establishing powerful large-scale associations, and the complicated physical features of south-eastern Europe did not exactly favour a union of several *župas* under one prince (*knez*). In later years, such separatism was only to be overcome, or mitigated, by pressure from outside.

The progressive weakening of the Avar kingdom after the middle of the seventh century had radically changed the balance of power in the Pannonian region. In their efforts to defend themselves against the destructive Avar invasions in the west, the dukedom of the Bavarians and its successor, the Carolingian empire, had found themselves drawn more and more into the affairs of the Danube region. But the rise of a new great Slav kingdom in 840, with its centre in Moravia and western Slovakia, the so-called Great Moravian empire of the Mojmirids, presented them with a powerful rival. At the beginning of the tenth century, it was to be destroyed by the invasion of the Magyars, who became the true successors to the Avars in the Danube-Tisza plain and founded a lasting empire. From this time on, the aspirations of the Hungarians to become a great power were to have far-ranging effects on the political life of the neighbouring Slav peoples.

During the Middle Ages a network of Balkan states eventually emerged out of this three-cornered struggle for power. The contestants were first, the eastern part of the Carolingian empire, i.e. the German empire of the Ottos, Salians and Hohenstaufen and the big landowners in the south-eastern provinces on the edge of the eastern Alps; second, in the north, the Great Moravian empire of the ninth century that became the Hungarian state ruled by the Arpadians up to 1301, by the Angevin dynasty from 1308 to 1382 and by Sigismund of Luxemburg from 1387 to 1437; and third, the Byzantine empire and its successor states after 1204 in the south.

The Bulgars were to follow the path of imperial expansion, too, and they incorporated large parts of the Balkan peninsula into their empire–which survived till the beginning of the eleventh century when it disintegrated before the renewed military strength of Byzantium. The first endeavours on the part of the Croats and the Serbs, however, between the ninth and twelfth centuries to build up an empire did not go much beyond the unification of various tribes. For tribal rivalries with constantly changing alliances confronted them at every stage. The change-over to a government with defined territorial boundaries was to be more successful in Bosnia in the later medieval period, and in the Serbian national state of the Nemanjici (1123–1394) and its continuation in the remnant states under the Lazarevići, the Brankovići and the despots in southern Hungary.

The Adriatic region only partially followed such a development.

The Roman provincial population, pushed back onto the islands by Slav settlers who had moved into the coastal towns, had looked for support from the Byzantine imperial navy and the rising commercial power of Venice: even during the peak period of Slav domination in the Balkans it preserved its special position, and it managed to maintain it in part during the period of Ottoman rule as well, as we shall see. Among the city republics along the Adriatic coast, Ragusa (Dubrovnik) was to remain until modern times the guardian of a proud freedom-loving tradition that permitted trade and commerce to flourish extensively.

The rise of the Bulgar-Slav state in the eastern zone of the Balkans towards the end of the seventh century had been much helped by the decline of the Byzantine defence system. The military triumphs of the emperor Heraclius against the hereditary Persian enemy had not given the Byzantine empire more than a few years of respite on the eastern front. Arab military pressure, which began after 632, had gathered strength and overwhelmed the eastern provinces, and then within a few years again broken down the Byzantine line of defence which had taken so long to rebuild. The provinces, but recently recaptured, were once more lost to the enemy. With their advanced military techniques, the Arabs had become a deadly menace to the empire. It was the caliph Muawiya (661–680) who had made the important decision to use the sea, a decision which was to have widespread consequences. For the creation of a separate Arab fleet gave him the necessary support to advance to the gates of Constantinople. Twice within a few score years the Byzantine capital had to defend itself against a severe Arab siege—in 674–678 and 717–718. Later, its defences were to be much weakened by the long and bitter quarrel, amounting to civil war, over the veneration of icons in the Orthodox Church, the 'iconoclastic' dispute of 730–843.[1]

---

[1] Iconoclast = literally 'image-breaker'. The name was used to describe a powerful party in the Byzantine empire which wished to suppress the use of icons. The attempt roused fierce opposition, and eventually failed. (Translator's note).

The new *theme*[1] system of defence, tried out in Asia Minor, had at first been ineffective in the Balkan peninsula in the face of these internal and external disasters and Slav aggression. The attempt had been made—as elsewhere in the empire—to create a uniform defence system and raise military forces from among the local population. This was to be done by general militarization of the provincial government, and by the allocation of land to conscripted soldiers in the threatened provinces. As the *theme* system was slowly introduced in the coastal areas of south-eastern Europe, Byzantium's reconquest of some of the lost lands became steadily more feasible.

In historical records the first mention of a *theme* is that of the Theme of Thrace in the year 687. At the turn of the century, Hellas and Macedonia were to become *themes*; and in the course of the ninth century, the remaining provincial governments, now merely nominal, were replaced by the Themes of Salonica, Strymon and Boleron. But only in the southern part of the Balkans did the Byzantine counter-offensive—conducted from the fortified coastal settlements to which the forces had retreated—with its planned restoration of Hellenic influence in the lowlands in the eighth century, have any permanent success. The turning point had come with the campaigns in mainland Greece and the Peloponnese of Stauracius, the able general of the empress Irene (797–802), and with the emperor Nicephorus I (802–811), who struck a decisive blow by capturing Patras in 805.

In the north, on the other hand, Byzantium had been unable to resist the Bulgars, who from their base in the Dobrudja had brought the surrounding Slav races—the Severians, in the so-called region of seven races—under their rule. In the next generations the small Bulgar upper class of Turco-Tatar extraction was to be swallowed up in the mass of the Slav population. The fusion of nomadic and peasant stocks was to contribute to the ending of racial separatism, and help introduce the Slav peasants in the eastern part of the peninsula to new forms of social and political life.

---

[1] A *theme* was a district headed by a military governor (*strategos*). The whole of the Byzantine empire was finally divided into *themes* for administrative purposes. (Translator's note).

Despite massive military and diplomatic intervention, mainly under the emperor Constantine V Copronymus (741–775), Byzantium was not able to arrest the development of separate states. At the beginning of the ninth century, the Bulgars found a gifted leader and statesman in Khan Krum (802–814), who had the courage to take on a war on two fronts–making a direct confrontation with the Franks in the west and Byzantium in the south–and so open the way for his people to supremacy in the inner Balkans and to extension of their empire. Krum took advantage of the Avar demise after the campaigns of Charles the Great, Pippin and the margrave Eric of Friuli in 791 and 795/6,[1] when the storming of the Avar ring in Alföld occurred, to incorporate into his empire the regions east of the Tisza, that is, east Pannonia. He then turned against Byzantium, and with the capture of Serdica (Sofia) in 809, his way was open to Thrace and Macedonia. In 811, Nicephorus failed to return from his campaign against the Bulgars; his army had been annihilated. Only her impregnable walls saved Constantinople two years later after the Bulgar victory at Versinikia in 813. Shortly before his sudden death in 814, Adrianople was also to fall into Krum's hands.

His successor Omortag (814–831) steered Byzantine-Bulgar relations into calmer channels, and agreed to a demarcation between their respective spheres of control which lasted for a period of thirty years. In the ten-year period of peace he created, Bulgaria was exposed to Hellenic cultural influences, and in the reign of Khan Boris to Christian missionaries as well.

The Slav races, most of them Croats and Serbs, who had settled in the provinces of Dalmatia and Pannonia, the former Roman province of Illyria, had been drawn into the struggles of their neighbours, being forced to take up positions and establish political alliances vis-à-vis the power groupings that were emerging. In particular, they had had to withstand fierce attacks from the Franks to the north-west, and Bulgar movements to the east.

[1] The diagonal stroke indicates discrepancies between the Julian and Gregorian calendars.

The Frankish advance into the Danube region after the Bavarian dukedom of Tassilos joined the empire in 788, the creation early in 776 of the Frankish margravate of Friuli, and the conquest of Istria, a Byzantine possession, had all helped to diminish the Avar threat. In the course of these ventures the Slav races of the eastern Alps, the Slovenes, who had been formed into the dukedom of Carantania and had been paying tribute to the Bavarian dukes since the middle of the eighth century, had been joined to the empire of the Franks. For an entire millennium after that, until the dissolution of the Austro-Hungarian Danubian monarchy in 1918, the Slovenes were to remain closely bound to the destiny of their German-speaking neighbours in Carinthia, Kranj and southern Styria.

The creation of the Pannonian or Eastern Marches and the Carinthian Marches in the year 803 was intended to ensure the security of Frankish acquisitions. In the process of suppressing the Avars, Charlemagne could count on the support of prince Vojnimir of Pannonia-Croatia, who had in fact merely exchanged the domination of the Avars for that of the Franks. Politically, he was subordinate to the margrave of Friuli, while ecclesiastical jurisdiction was exercised in his region by the patriarch of Aquileia. By an arbitration of 811, the diocesan boundaries in Carantania between Aquileia and Salzburg were to be fixed along the river Drava.

Despite all these arrangements, peace had not yet been firmly established among the Slavs of Pannonia. In 819, the Slav Ljudevit led a revolt against the Franks which Louis the Pious was only able to crush in 822 after several campaigns. But later on, prince Pribina, who had been ousted from his ancestral dominions around Nitra by the Moravian prince Mojmir, and had arrived in Pannonia, was to prove himself a true vassal and servant of the Franks; here between Lake Balaton, the Sava and the Danube, Louis gave him a new political task which he solved with skill. He was to fall in battle against the Magyars in 861, and his son Kocel then continued his work for more than a decade (861–876).

As well as warding off enemies, these two and other Slav princes managed to bring peace to the Pannonian region by their policy of planned resettlement, their intelligent programme of reconstruction, and the conversion of its inhabitants to Christianity. Under their auspices there was an influx of German settlers, who, in addition to establishing the Christian mission in Salzburg, contributed much to the development of the land; and with the help of German artists and craftsmen the residence of prince Pribina at Moosburg (Zalavár) on Lake Balaton became a new cultural centre. This, however, did not survive the invasion of the Magyars towards the end of the ninth century, as we have seen.

The suppression of the Ljudevit rising was to bring Louis the Pious temporarily into conflict with the Bulgars, and their territorial demands gave rise to fighting for another ten years or more (827–838). It was not till developments in the north threatened the region towards the middle of the century that the two parties combined their forces and formed an alliance. Prince Rastislav of Moravia, once a supporter of Louis the Pious, had become a passionate protagonist of Moravian separatism and its strivings towards independence. His expansionist ideas were a threat to the claims of both Franks and Bulgars. So the Bulgar Khan Boris (852–889) had changed his foreign policy: he had drawn closer to the Franks, hoping to win their support against the uprisings encouraged by Byzantine diplomacy of the Slav races in the western Balkans.

After the death of Omortag in 831, the Bulgarian advance to the Ohrid and Prespa lakes in Macedonia had given new impetus to Byzantium's defensive and diplomatic activity, and Arab operations in the Adriatic had also alerted her to the need for allies. Help came unexpectedly. In 862, Rastislav sent a delegation to the Byzantine court asking for Christian missionaries and proposing a political alliance. This change in Moravian religious policy meant that Franco-Bavarian missionaries were no longer welcome and was a natural consequence of Rastislav's new political position. In the same way, the Bulgar Khan Boris had wanted to ensure that the now inevitable conversion of his people to Christianity would be brought about under the auspices of distant Rome rather than those of nearby Constantinople.

A pagan state in a Christian environment which had accepted the idea of missionaries as part of its foreign policy had no chance of survival. Even if it made occasional agreements with the more politically minded Christian potentates, its ability to form alliances would be open to question. Because of Christianity's militancy towards other religions, there would be no guaranteed basis for international agreements. The official conversion to Christianity, then, was motivated more by power-politics than theology. For in spite of mutual reservations about special developments, the western and eastern churches had not yet reached such a point of rivalry in founding new missionary areas that central matters of the faith had been affected. The Roman church had at that time by no means closed its mind to accepting the Slav language as the language of the liturgy, for instance. Existing differences and the resulting political groupings had given opportunities for arranging the new church organizations into areas of ecclesiastical jurisdiction. Both Rastislav of Moravia and the Bulgar Khan Boris made use of the situation and tried to extract themselves from political complications threatening them by calculated shifts in their religious loyalties.

In reply to Rastislav's request, the far-sighted patriarch Photius (858–867 and 877–886) sent out two Greek missionaries, both of them language scholars, the brothers Cyril (Constantine) and Methodius, in 863. It was a decision of great consequence for the Byzantine church, though these 'Apostles of the Slavs' had no enduring success in distant Moravia. The Bavarian church, jealously guarding its rights, had recovered from its period of setbacks, and was resisting penetration by the Greek church through a series of ecclesiastical and political counter-measures. Of great importance to the entire Slav world, however, was the magnificent work of translation by the two brothers. They had presented Slav missionaries with the most important Christian writings and liturgical works in a language understood by all Slavs—the so-called Church-Slavonic, an ancient south Slav dialect which the brothers had learned from Slav settlers in the hinterland of Salonica.

The first country where the works of the Slav teachers took firm root was Bulgaria. Here Khan Boris offered the disciples of Cyril and Methodius, who had fled from Moravia in 885, a new field of operation. In 865, Khan Boris had been baptized into the Byzantine church and had taken the name Michael from his royal godfather. Military demonstrations on the part of the Byzantines had undoubtedly made this decision easier for him. But it had not been till 870 that he had in the end abandoned his intention of building up a church organization under a Roman bishop independent of Byzantium. Towards the end of the century, his son Simeon was to succeed in winning back his power over the church by creating a separate Bulgarian patriarchate.

Boris-Michael had to establish Christianity by brute force against the opposition of the heathen nobility and their supporters in the dwindling groups of original Bulgars. As in other regions, here too conversion to Christianity made an important contribution in the establishment of a state and the consolidation of the power of its prince. Boris-Michael's voluntary renunciation of the throne when he became a monk and retreated to a monastery in 888 leaving his eldest son Vladimir (889–893) to rule, temporarily endangered his work. In 893 he felt compelled to return, in order to defend his country from a pagan reactionary movement. Vladimir's brilliance, which was matched by that of his younger brother who was to replace him, paved the way for the golden age of Bulgarian medieval history at the turn of the tenth century. An attempt was made to challenge Byzantium's rule in the central Balkan countries. The struggle between Byzantium and the Bulgars was to overshadow the whole historical development of south-eastern Europe for several generations.

The differences between Byzantium and the Bulgars, which were becoming more marked, were paralleled in the north-west of the peninsula by disagreements between Byzantium and the Franks. There had only been direct and lasting Byzantine influence over Slav races in the area along the Adriatic coast where the presence of a strong navy had given support to Byzantine claims. The advance of the Franks towards the Adriatic violating Byzantine sovereignty, as for instance with their occupation of Istria in 788, and the coronation of Charlemagne in Rome on Christmas day 800–which was regarded as an insult–had thus increased the danger of large-scale conflict between the two empires. In 803, a boundary in the Dalmatian area was fixed, separating their spheres of influence. By the treaty of Königshofen, Venice, the islands and the coastal towns were left to Byzantium, and the inland regions were given to the empire of the Franks. The acquisition of Venice and the Dalmatian towns a few years later in 806 and 810 then gave Charlemagne a temporary advantage, but when in 812 he secured from the emperor Michael I in Aachen the recognition of his title of 'emperor' (of the west), it was in return for restoration of the status quo.

The revolt of the Pannonian Slavs against Frankish rule and the Franco-Bulgarian-Byzantine quarrels in the first half of the ninth century were to have an effect on the Slav races in the north-western part of the Balkans. The gradual rise of native princes had begun in the hilly regions in the interior. By steering a middle course between the powers, they had succeeded in strengthening and enlarging their area of rule, and the ineffectiveness of the official supreme authority had made it easier for Byzantine diplomacy to encourage these efforts to achieve independence and give them an anti-Bulgarian slant. The Serbian tribes from the area of Raška (Rascia)–in the upper valleys of the rivers Tara, Piva and Lim (tributaries of the Drina) and the Ibar–who had been led to independence for a short period by Vlastimir, successfully defended themselves in the first three decades of the ninth century against further expansion of the Bulgars to the west. But it was more difficult for the Slavs in the coastal areas, the Croats, to make political capital out of the temporary weakness of the Byzantine empire in the Adriatic region. In the north, Frankish policy was able to secure the loyalty of a number of princes through a system of federal relationships. With the appearance in 867 of Arab fleet formations before Ragusa, the peoples in the coastal areas had found themselves forced to return to the protection of Byzantium and its imperial fleet. So that the emperor Basil I (867–886)–after his short-lived successes in Bulgaria–had managed to open up the western part of the Balkans to Byzantine influence once again. The activities of Methodius' disciples in

Macedonia and Bulgaria sent a last wave of Hellenic influence far into the west before the results of the Byzantine-Bulgar feud that began around the turn of the century cleared the way for new developments.

4

THE STRUGGLE FOR SUPREMACY
IN THE BALKAN INTERIOR
BETWEEN BYZANTIUM AND THE
BULGARS

By the turn of the tenth century, the transformation of the eastern part of the Frankish empire into the German empire was complete. In the Danube region, internal upheavals were temporarily of greater importance. Byzantium, having overcome the iconoclastic conflict, was beginning to reassemble its forces against outside aggression. Two series of events were now to cause radical change in south-eastern Europe: the annexation of land by the Magyars after 895, and the successful political moves of the Bulgarian tsar Simeon (893–927). The events were not unrelated. Following a well-established pattern, Byzantium diplomacy had in 894 secured Magyar support against Bulgarian threats, and this move had prompted the Bulgarian ruler to ally himself with the Pechenegs who lived on the far side of the Magyars. To escape the pressure of the Pechenegs, the Magyars in 896 moved westwards across the Carpathians into the Danube-Tisza plain. In 906 the Pechenegs had struck a death blow to the Moravian empire. The defence line established in the east Bavarian province under margrave Luitpold had been unable to halt the furious assault of the mounted nomadic troops. Neither Luitpold nor any of the Bavarian hereditary nobility who followed him were to return from the bloody battle of Pressburg on July 4th, 907.

The annexation of lands by the Magyars—who were of Finno-Ugrian origin though they had assimilated a strong Turkic element during their long period of migration to the west—is traditionally linked with the person of Arpád. Himself a Magyar, he is remembered in history as the founder of the first Arpadian ruling dynasty, which lasted till 1301, and he is said to have led seven nomad Magyar tribes together with Chazarian splinter groups into the Pannonian plain. It was not until the German victory under the leadership of Otto I on the battlefield of Lech on August 10th, 955, that the years of devastation were brought to an end. The German empire was not alone in finding the Magyars uncomfortable neighbours. Byzantium also suffered from continuous attacks by Magyar hordes. In 934 and 959, they advanced to the walls of Constantinople. However, as they changed from a nomadic to a settled way of life and created a unified nation, it became possible for them to develop peaceful relations with their neighbours.

Although king Stephen I (997–1038), the saint and the husband of the Bavarian princess Gisela of the house of Luidolfinger, was to follow in the tradition of his father Géza, and direct his country towards western civilization, he did not sever all communications with the Byzantine world. The new common frontier resulting from the elimination of the Bulgarian empire at the beginning of the eleventh century made contact easier, and the conclusion of a number of military alliances during the eleventh century and at the beginning of the twelfth strengthened their common interests. Towards the middle of the twelfth century, the idea that had been mooted for a union of the two dynasties looked like becoming a reality. The son of Géza II (1141–1162), who had been brought up at the Byzantine palace and who was later to become king Béla III of Hungary (1173–1196), was chosen as heir to the Byzantine throne and was married to Maria, the daughter of the emperor Manuel I. But even Byzantine involvement on a grand scale in the quarrels of the Hungarian throne could not in the long run smooth out the differences that had arisen between them in the struggle for domination in the northern Balkans. The advance of the Hungarians beyond the Danube-Sava line towards the Adriatic coast, to Croatia and Dalmatia, was never re-examined when Byzantine supremacy over that region was recognized by treaty in 1167. So, while trying to solve the urgent Bulgarian question at the end of the ninth century, Byzantium had invited into the land its most serious rival for power in the Balkan interior: the future was to belong with the Hungarians.

Tsar Simeon, in spite of the earlier embarrassment he had had from the Magyar allies of the emperor Leo VI (886–912), was to conclude the latest clash of arms between the Bulgars and Byzantium, that had had its origin in differences over trade policy, with a brilliant victory at Bulgarophygon in 896. He knew how to turn his hard-won victory to account. The unexpected capture of Salonica by an Arab naval expedition on July 31st, 904, was to help him to make further frontier adjustments. Then barely ten years later, the offhand attitude adopted by the new Byzantine government after the death of Leo VI in 912 towards the payments agreed on at the treaty of 896 provoked him to a devastating military campaign, and for a time he brought the Byzantine empire to the brink of destruction.

Twice, in 913 and 924, Simeon's mighty army, too, had stood outside the gates of Constantinople. In 914 Adrianople had fallen. Even the queen mother Zoe, who had returned after the end of the regency of the patriarch Nicholas Mysticus, had not been able to put up any substantial resistance, and on August 20th, 917, she had suffered a crushing defeat at Acheloos. Only the walls of Constantinople had defied the great Bulgarian tsar. However, he was never to achieve his ambition of becoming ruler of a Byzantine-Bulgarian empire. For he died suddenly on May 27th, 927. It is true that in 913 Nicholas Mysticus had granted him a ceremonial entry into Constantinople where he had been crowned–'Basileus of the Bulgars', though not 'of the Romans'–but the undertaking of further obligations had been strictly refused him by Zoe's government. In the last event, when his wish to become emperor of the Romans had almost been achieved, he had been forestalled by Romanus Lecapenus, the former *drungarios* or commander of the imperial navy. In 919, as father-in-law of the emperor Constantine VII Porphyrogenitus, Romanus had taken the title of Basileopater, and in 920 he had confirmed his position by making himself Caesar and co-emperor. Under these circumstances, Simeon's self-adopted title of 'emperor of the Romans and Bulgars' had carried no weight. His Bulgarian empire stretching from the Adriatic to the Black Sea and as far as Salonica and Constantinople was deprived of that final achievement. With his death ended the first period Bulgaria was to experience as a great power. His son and successor, Peter (927–969), had to be satisfied with the Bulgarian title of *basileus* at the conclusion of peace in 927, and with having the hand in marriage of Maria Lecapena, the grand-daughter of Romanus I.

In the history of medieval Bulgaria, the reign of Simeon was not only a period of glory for its foreign policy; it was also the golden age of early Bulgarian literature. The literary language had been developed by the 'apostles of the Slavs', Cyril and Methodius, and by their disciples, who had continued their work on Bulgarian territory. This language was used in the excellent translations of Kliment of Ohrid, bishop Constantine of Preslav (Konstantin Presbyter) and the exarch John, whose main work *Hexameron* was a compilation from Greek sources and included a vivid description of Simeon's residence in the capital, Preslav. It was during the reign of tsar Peter that the *Apologia for the Slav Languages* by the monk Chrabr and the propaganda tracts against the Bogomils of the priest Cosmas were written. Cultural life in Bulgaria was to follow the Byzantine example closely, and find its visible expression in the ostentatious furnishings of the rulers' residences in Preslav and Ohrid. The Byzantine influence reached its peak in Peter's reign, by which time the decline of the proud empire was already becoming evident.

Years of military clashes with Byzantium and its Hungarian, Serbian and Croatian allies had exhausted the country's strength, and long-harboured social grievances threatened to come out into the open. Behind the surprising success of the radical, anti-clerical and anti-hierarchical movement of the Bogomil sect, which had had growing support among the lower strata of the population, had lain a massive protest against the established order in church and state. In taking up ancient Manichean ideas stemming from Asia Minor, Bulgaria was to introduce a new and fertile element into medieval religious thought, and not only in the Balkan countries. For later sectarian movements of the Middle Ages in the west such as the Cathars, Albigenses and others also showed its influence; indeed, there are many strands of sectarian thought with Balkan origins. Bulgaria and Bosnia were the two main points of contact between oriental gnostic-Manichean and heretical-Christian ideas. Medieval Bulgaria had, therefore, a unique position as a cultural go-between, passing on to the Orthodox Slavs literary translations into church-Slavonic as well as elements of Byzantine culture and sectarian ideas. In fact, Bulgaria's influence in the cultural life of the Balkan peoples was to prove more lasting than her success in creating a nation.

It was in the second half of the tenth century that the Byzantine empire put an end to the Bulgarian state after acquiring new strength from its victorious campaigns against the Arabs—from its conquest of Crete in 961 and of Aleppo in 962, the capital of Emir Saif-ad-Daulah of Mosul and Aleppo; the victorious march after 963 of the emperor Nicephorus II Phocas (963–969) through Cilicia to Syria; and the conquest of Antioch on October 28th, 969. At first, Nicephorus had left the military subjection of Bulgaria to the warlike Russian prince of Kiev, Sviatoslav, who in two campaigns in 967–968 had forced tsar Peter and his son Boris II (969–972) to surrender, and had occupied the land without giving any consideration to Byzantine claims. Sviatoslav had even considered moving his residence from the Dnieper to the north-east of the Balkans. A large-scale military expedition had been required before the new emperor John I Tzimisces (969–976) had been able wrest back from him what he had gained. Only when he had renounced all his conquests had the Russian prince been allowed to leave the beleaguered province of Silistria on the Danube and return to the Dnieper—where he fell shortly afterwards in a skirmish with the Pechenegs. During these Byzantine operations, Bulgaria lost not merely her political independence but in addition the centre of her national church, the Bulgarian patriarchate. The historical importance of these events can scarcely be over-estimated. After three hundred years, Byzantium had once more succeeded in pushing her frontiers forward as far as the Danube in the eastern part of the Balkan peninsula.

In the central Balkans, however, the restoration of Byzantine rule was to meet with considerable opposition. For under the four Cometopuli brothers, the sons of the governor (*comes*) Nicholas of western Bulgaria, that is, Macedonia, a rebel movement grew up after 976 and finally became a threat to the power that had just been won back by Byzantium. The youngest of the brothers, Samuel, was a particular danger. Operating from his capital Prespa, and later from Ohrid, he revived the Great Bulgarian Empire, so recently fallen into decline, and gave the Bulgarian church a new focal point in the patriarchate of Ohrid. After an unsuccessful advance against Serdica (Sofia) in 986, the emperor Basil II (976–1025) was badly defeated by him. His hands were then tied by the outbreak of a civil war–caused by the uprisings of Bardas Scleros and afterwards Bardas Phocas in 987–989–and new entanglements in the east in Syria and the Caucasus. However, from 1001 onwards he took personal command of military operations in the Balkans and, after a guerilla campaign conducted in 1014 with unparalleled grimness, eventually struck a fatal blow against Samuel. At the Kleidion pass (Klunč), the Bulgarian tsar lost the greater part of his army. The Bulgarian prisoners, who were estimated at between fourteen and fifteen thousand, were all blinded by Basil and sent back to Samuel in Prilep where he had retreated. Unable to stand the dreadful spectacle, he died on October 6th, 1014. His son, Gabriel Radomir, only outlived him by a year, for in 1015 he was murdered by John Vladislav, Samuel's nephew, who seized what remained of Bulgaria. John's death at Dyrrhachium (Durazzo) in 1018 was to open the gates of Ohrid to the emperor. In 1019, the 'Bulgar-slayer', the *Bulgaroktonos*, returned in a triumphal march through Athens to Constantinople.

The Byzantine empire had, after a series of grandiose conquests, recaptured a final glimmer of its world prestige and brought back under its control the greater part of the Balkans. The development of the *theme* organization was to ensure the future division of power, and a cleverly organized system of vassal states curbed the Serbs' and Croats' desires for independence, binding them to the empire. For the last time, Byzantium had extended its influence as far as the Adriatic. The great work of restoration was not to survive for long.

In the eleventh century, the position of the empire was seriously shaken. The Seljuk Turks emerged in the east and the Normans in

Map 6. The Byzantine empire in the tenth century

the west in Sicily; the nomadic peoples of the steppes of Central Asia, the Pechenegs, the Uzes and the Cumans were to make devastating forays across the lower Danube into the interior of the Balkans; and the western Crusades started. These events brought new disturbing factors into Balkan political life, and, especially in the north-west, helped bring to a head a development that had started as early as the ninth century: the growth in power of the Serbs and Croats. Just as in the case of the Magyars, Byzantine diplomacy had had to pay the price for its anti-Bulgarian campaign, and that price was a growing political consciousness among the leaders of other peoples striving for independence.

Circumstances were first favourable for the Croats on Dalmatian territory who were subject to the margrave of Friuli and the Carolingians in Italy. They had at the end of the ninth century taken advantage of the absence of the Franks since 875, and had in a large-scale rebellion thrown off in a few years the last vestiges of Frankish domination. The true founder of independent Croatia was prince Branimir (879–892), who had come to the fore when he had opposed the pro-Byzantine politics of Zdeslav (878–879).

The Roman form of Christianity had already taken root in the Dalmatian cities in the seventh century and in the Frankish-dominated Croatian hinterland at the turn of the ninth century. A separate church organization with its centre in the archbishopric of Spalato (Split), bypassing the old bishopric at Nin, had been created by the patriarchate of Aquileia. The suppression of the use of the vernacular with glagolitic characters in the Slavonic church service was to provoke much dissension in church politics. This Slavonic service had been the result of the missionary work of Cyril and Methodius, and had also spread among the Croats along the littoral. Many local synods had had to accept it and had been unable to enforce the Roman liturgy. In some outlying regions the Slavonic church service survived for centuries, and prayer books in glagolitic script still bear witness today to the cultural history of the Croatian-Dalmatian coastal region.

At the turn of the tenth century, the Dalmatian part of Croatia was well on its way to achieving hegemony over the western

Balkans, as the result of planned expansion. The invasion of the Magyars, which temporarily involved prince Tomislav around 910–928 in border disputes in the north, could not alter the situation, and the Croatian expansion continued unhalted in the Pannonian area. Only Syrmia and eastern Slavonia were to come under Magyar rule. The differences between Byzantium and tsar Simeon favoured the formation of a Croatian state. While Simeon had dealt with the Serbs, who had been encouraged to rebel by Byzantine diplomacy in about 924, in a successful campaign, and had brought their whole area within the orbit of his empire, he had suffered a crushing defeat at the hands of the Croats, and had had to agree to peace conditions laid down by the pope. It was Rome, too, who subsequently in 924 sanctioned prince Tomislav's royal title and thereby gave prestige to the newly-formed state. Tomislav ended up by ruling over north and south Dalmatia (i.e. White and Red Croatia), parts of the neighbouring islands, and Istria and Bosnia. He also ensured himself considerable influence in the neighbouring regions of Travunia, Dioclea and Zachumlia (see pages 67 and 84). Thanks to his large navy, he was able to hold his own in the Adriatic against Venice and Byzantium as well.

But his successors could not maintain the territorial stability of this new kingdom. Experience had taught that it was not except with the support of a neighbouring great power that a successful campaign could be conducted against the separatist tendencies of the chieftains of local tribes. Stefan Držislav (969–997), a hardened diplomat, was to be closely associated with the Byzantine emperor Basil II in suppressing the Cometopuli rebellion, and to confirm his position of power in Dalmatia. In nominating him exarch of Dalmatia, Byzantium gave him possession of towns and islands in the former Byzantine Theme of Dalmatia, and finally recognized his position as king with a grant of royal insignia in 986.

The strengthening of Venice and Hungary, the two powers on Croatia's borders, ended any possibilities of further expansion. Even open declarations of papal support failed to prevent the 'regnum Dalmatiae et Chroatiae' from being crushed between the two power blocs in the next century. In 1000, the Dalmatian cities fell to the Venetians. After the death of the capable Peter Krešimir IV (1058–1074), Demetrius Zvonimir–the 'Ban' of Pannonian Croatia–was unable to reverse the trend. With the support of pope Gregory VII he had had himself crowned king in 1076, and through his wife Helen, a sister of Géza I, he had been able to maintain good relations with his neighbour Hungary. The medieval kingdom of Croatia eventually crumbled after the murder of Zvonimir in 1089 because the tribal princes could not agree on a successor to the throne or put an end to the chaos in the country that almost amounted to civil war.

Hungary knew how to make the best of the situation. Supported by a pro-Hungarian group among the Croatian aristocracy, king Ladislas I (1077–1095) was called into the land. In systematic military campaigns, he and his successor, Koloman, proceeded to conquer Croatia step by step and break down all local resistance to Hungarian rule. Peter Svačić, the Dalmatian leader, who had, with Venetian and Norman support, since 1091 organized the bitter resistance all along the coast to the advancing Hungarians, was killed in a decisive battle at Petrova Gora in 1097. A union between the Hungarian and Croatian kingdoms was established on a firm treaty basis in 1102 by king Koloman after negotiations between the Croatian aristocracy and the twelve tribes, whose privileges he guaranteed. The historical and legal meaning of this so-called 'Pacta conventa' is still much debated by Hungarian and Croatian historians and publicists since historical records indicate that the union actually took effect a whole century later.

The threefold kingdom of Dalmatia, Croatia and Slavonia was to retain its social structure and laws under Arpadian rule, the administration and the army remaining in the hands of the ruling classes. The newly acquired territories were added to the title of the king of Hungary, who became 'Dei Gratia rex Hungariae, Chroatiae atque Dalmatiae', but in the country itself the Croatian 'Ban' representing the king, together with the assembly, the *sabor*, protected national autonomy and the privileged position held by the aristocracy. From then on Croatia's destiny was closely linked with that of Hungary and, up to 1918, with that of the later Austro-Hungarian Habsburg monarchy.

In the early Middle Ages the Serbian tribes had to battle against far greater difficulties than the Croatian ones in their struggle for national independence. Throughout the ninth and tenth centuries, individual tribal princes had succeeded for a time in holding their own against Byzantium, and against their powerful Bulgarian neighbour to the east who had since the days of Simeon encroached on Serbian territory. In 931, prince Časlav had taken advantage of a period of weakness in Bulgaria under tsar Peter, and led a new and not unsuccessful attempt at rebellion. However, his successes barely outlived him. In the second half of the tenth century, the Serbian tribes had again come under the influence of Samuel's west Bulgarian kingdom, but with its subsequent decline Byzantine supremacy was restored.

Byzantium, operating from secure bases on the coast, had tried to secure the allegiance of the vassal tribes in the interior; the purely formal nature of the relationship, though, was shown up in about 1035 when prince Stefan Vojslav had renounced his allegiance in the coastal region of Zeta, formerly Dioclea (the present Montenegro together with north Albania, and in particular the country around the lake of Scutari). After surviving imprisonment in Constantinople, he had defied all punitive expeditions from Byzantium. He had also supported the serious Slav rebellion under Peter Delian in the central Balkans in 1040/41 and helped him extend his influence among the neighbouring Serbian tribes. The principality of Zeta had looked like becoming the nucleus of an independent Serbian national state, bringing the individual Serbian lands under common rule.

The coastal region had fallen fairly quickly to Stefan Vojslav and he had conquered Trebinje (Travunia, between Cattaro and Ragusa) as well as Zachumlia (the 'country beyond the hills', Zahumlje) where prince Michael, 'Dux Chulmorum', had on several occasions in the tenth century proved himself an independent politician. Stefan Vojslav's son and successor, Michael (c. 1050–1082), managed to win the support of the Roman Curia for his country's progress and–like Demetrius Zvonimir in Croatia–he received the title of king from pope Gregory VII. Political concessions to the church of Rome were the price to be paid for these promotions. Bar (Antivari) was raised to an archbishopric and became the centre of the Serbian Catholic church. Stefan's second son, Constantine Bodin (1082–1100), who had led a revolt of the Slav population in Macedonia against Byzantium in 1072, and had got himself elected tsar at Prizren, rounded off the task of uniting the Serbian tribes by taking over Bosnia and Raška. After his death, there was nobody at all to carry on his political programme, which folded up under the incompetence of his successors.

Because of disagreements within the dynasty, the border areas were soon to fall away again; so that the attempt to unite the Slav peoples that had started under Latin auspices in the western coastal regions failed, in spite of a promising start at the beginning of the twelfth century. A second attempt was made half a century later in the eastern mountain regions, and this time it was a success. External political conditions at and after the end of the twelfth century had been favourable because, after collapsing in 1204 during the fourth Crusade, the Byzantine empire had no longer been a restraining influence in the development of relations between the Balkan peoples and its heirs had relied on new powers from the border areas. The Balkan peninsula ceased to be a political unit, and broke up into a number of local formations. The sea power of Venice was coming to the fore in the Adriatic, and the kingdom of Hungary was pushing down from the north into Croatian-Bosnian-Serbian territory. The rise of the Nemanjici in Serbia and that of the Asenids in Bulgaria, producing the 'Second Bulgarian Empire', was to lead to a new phase in Balkan political history in which the Byzantine empire surrendered its leading role.

5

THE RISE OF VENICE AND THE CREATION OF THE INDEPENDENT STATES OF SERBIA AND BULGARIA

In a natural shift in the balance of power, Venice succeeded in the eleventh century to Byzantium's control of the Adriatic coast. Protected by her lagoons, Venice had been growing into a leading centre of commerce since 452, when she had given refuge to Romans fleeing from Attila's Huns after the battle of Rialto. Her merchant ships dominated the Adriatic and carried on trade as far as the eastern Mediterranean, Venetians controlling an important part of the trade with the Balkan interior, where they had a salt monopoly and organized timber exports and imports of luxury goods. The early establishment of good relations with the Arabs, the rulers of the eastern Mediterranean, had given her considerable trade advantages over other Italian coastal towns. The slave trade in particular had become a lucrative undertaking.

When, in the ninth century, internal unrest and conditions resembling civil war had shaken the Byzantine empire and weakened its hold over the Adriatic coast, Venice had found herself forced to protect more and more the freedom of the seas for merchant ships threatened by piratical Slav tribes in the coastal areas. The armistice made with the Narentans, a warlike, plundering Slav tribe who arrived at Venice in 830 in the time of the doge John Patricianus, had been short-lived. But through punitive expeditions Venice had been able to ward off the attacks of the Narentans and Croatians in the 830s and 840s. In the middle of the century, the Saracens had also begun to launch surprise attacks on Adriatic coastal towns from their newly-gained key position in Sicily. This had stimulated the rapid building of a Venetian navy, which was gradually to reduce the military importance of the Byzantine imperial fleet.

In the following decades, Venice learnt to safeguard her growing independence by a careful policy of playing off the western and eastern empires against each other, and to guarantee for herself certain strategic advantages by superior naval power. The 'birthday' of Venetian supremacy in the Adriatic is generally considered to have been marked by the great naval expedition of Pietro Orseolo II in 1000; this achieved the first substantial territorial gains from the Slav tribes living on the coast of Istria and Dalmatia. During their efforts to dominate the vital littoral of Dalmatia in the eleventh century, the Venetians and Byzantines were confronted with new claimants to the area. The daring leap of the Normans from southern Italy to southern Dalmatia was a formidable threat to the freedom of the seas in the Adriatic: the closing of the route from Otranto became a distinct possibility. Their alliance with the Byzantines in this crisis, born of necessity, was to bring the Venetians lasting benefits. In return for military assistance they were able to negotiate a treaty that opened up the whole of the Byzantine empire to Venetian trade, free of customs and duties. It was secured by the Chrysobull of 1082. However, some further token of goodwill was demanded. Victory over the Norman fleet at Dyrrhachium failed to achieve the expected results, as the emperor Alexius I Comnenus (1081–1118) had been unable to relieve the city from the mainland. In October 1081, Robert Guiscard forced Dyrrhachium to surrender, but the Venetians took it back only a year later. The immediate threat had been averted, not so much by the continued operations of the two allies, which had achieved disappointingly little, as by an unforeseen piece of luck; a terrible epidemic of the plague was to decimate the Norman army and carry off Guiscard, its leader, in 1085.

Of greater consequence than the Norman episode had been the Hungarian kings' pressure to gain free access to the Adriatic, because it had prevented the Venetians from building up an overseas empire. Even in the 1040s and 1050s, the Hungarians had been making successful incursions into Croatian-Dalmatian territory, and they had been able to consolidate them, too. Family connections with the dying Croatian ruling dynasty had provided the basis for their policy of expansion. When the Hungarian kings had finally confronted the rival power, Venice had only been able to maintain her authority in the coastal cities, her rightful ownership of them being subsequently confirmed by Byzantium. Generous guarantees of privileges by the Hungarian kings brought many cities over to their side. For centuries to come, the rivalry between Venice and Hungary was to determine policies along the Adriatic littoral. It began with a number of military incidents starting in 1115; it was taken over by the Habsburgs; and it did not come to an end until the fall of the Venetian republic in 1797.

At the beginning of the twelfth century, the Byzantine emperors came to see that the one-sided privileges extended to Venetian trade were having disastrous consequences. Radical counter-measures such as the withdrawal of privileges in 1124, the confiscation of property, and the arrest of every Venetian living on imperial territory on St. George's Day (12th March) 1171 proved ineffective and were rescinded under Venetian pressure. The freedom of action in foreign policy so far enjoyed by the Byzantine empire was fast disappearing, and in spite of some military successes, Byzantium in the end lost control of the Balkan peninsula in the twelfth century, as we have seen in chapter 4.

Unmistakable evidence of this new direction in foreign affairs had been provided in the fatal year of 1071 when at the battle of Manzikert in Armenia Byzantium had suffered a crushing defeat at the hands of the advancing Seljuks, and had at the same time had to abandon Bari, its last stronghold in southern Italy, to the Normans. The work of restoration of the great Comneni emperors (1081–1185) did no more than delay the decline. The Latin conquest of Constantinople in 1204 during the Fourth Crusade, which the doge Enrico had diverted from its true aims in pursuit of a purely Venetian political objective, was the last chapter in a drama that had continued for several centuries. As a result, Balkan history was finally to take a separate course, independent of the empire. The region was to break up into a number of small rival domains that dominated the scene until a new phase of imperialism followed the conquests of the Ottoman empire.

* * *

71

In the second half of the twelfth century, both the Bulgarian and Serbian peoples succeeded in achieving independence almost simultaneously. The political awakening of the Serbian mountain regions around the upper courses of the Tara, Piva, Lim and Ibar rivers–the area of the former Raška–had begun at the end of the eleventh century immediately after the failure of the attempt at unification made by the prince of Zeta. The Serbian Župans had found a natural ally in their neighbour, Hungary, and with Hungarian support had been able to resist repeated Byzantine expeditions against them. The renunciation of allegiance by the Grand Župan, Stefan Nemanja, in 1166 or 1167 was, however, premature. For in 1172 the emperor Manuel I Comnenus (1143–1180) succeeded in re-establishing the allegiance of the vassal states by force. But his death in 1180 and a renewed Norman advance into the Balkans leading to the battle of Dyrrhachium in June 1185 and the capture of Salonica on August 24th of the same year were to ensure the withdrawal of Byzantine pressure. Already in 1181 the Hungarian king Béla III had won back the areas Hungary had lost to Byzantium in 1167, i.e. Dalmatia, Croatia and the Syrmian area; and a Hungaro-Serbian military alliance had threatened to end Andronicus Comnenus' reign of terror in 1183.

Stefan Nemanja seized this moment to secure Serbian independence, and enlarge his domains. In particular, he reinforced the leading position of Raška in relation to other Serbian regions thereby protecting the area from the prince of Zeta's political ambitions. When he voluntarily renounced the throne in 1196–going first into retreat at a monastery he had built in Studenica, and eventually retiring to Mount Athos–he left behind him an internally strong kingdom that was to hold its own during the tumultuous thirteenth century and in time become the prime Balkan power.

But before that, the 'Second Bulgarian Empire' was to rise spectacularly in the eastern Balkans. In 1185, the brothers Peter (Theodore) and Asen, with strong support from the Vlachs and the Cumans, led a successful revolt against the hated Byzantine rule. It had been a particularly hard blow for Byzantium as it had only just won a victory over the Normans at Dimitrica on November 7th, 1185, after which the Normans had retreated from Salonica and Dyrrhachium. The emperor Isaac II Angelus (1185–1195) had at first succeeded in pushing the rebellious Bulgarian leaders back across the Danube. The arrival, though, of considerable Cuman reinforcements and the support of Stefan Nemanja had compelled him to agree to an independent Bulgaria, whose territorial rights were to be limited to the areas between the lower Danube and the Balkan mountain ranges.

The threat to Byzantium that the two new powers of Serbia and Bulgaria had created in the Balkans soon became apparent when, during the Crusade of 1189, Stefan Nemanja and the Bulgarians openly opposed Byzantium and entered into an alliance with the emperor Frederick Barbarossa. Once the critical situation created by the Crusaders' army had been dealt with, a show of force by the Byzantines had more success against the Serbians than the Bulgarians, who had found in Kalojan (1197–1207), brother of Peter and Asen, an effective and ambitious leader. Kalojan had, since 1204, worn the crown he had received at Trnovo from pope Innocent III at the hands of cardinal Leo. On the day before the splendid coronation ceremony the cardinal consecrated archbishop Basil Trnovo as the new head of the Bulgarian church. Under Roman auspices there began a final period of glory for medieval Bulgaria. Within a few decades the struggle of the Second Bulgarian Empire for the succession to the capital city on the Bosphorus, after its fall in 1204, had gained surprising dimensions. But the sober and purposeful policy of the Serbian Nemanjas were in the end to force Bulgaria to yield the leadership of the central Balkans to them.

The rise of Serbia to a position of leadership began at the beginning of the thirteenth century with the sons of Stefan Nemanja – Stefan Prvovenčani (the First-crowned) and his brother, Rastko-Sava, who had taken holy orders. A strong sense of realism, characteristic of so many members of the house of Nemanja, enabled Stefan to counter the attempts of his elder brother, Vukan, to usurp his crown. With papal and Hungarian help, Vukan did temporarily fight his way to the throne from his stronghold of Zeta in 1203. But he turned out to be no match for his brother's skilful manoeuvrings between Rome, Bulgaria and Hungary. In 1217, Stefan accepted a crown from the hands of the pope. However, he left the solution of immediate ecclesiastical problems to his brother Sava, whose aim was the establishment of an Orthodox Serbian national church in defiance of the wishes of the Roman see, and who negotiated with the Greek patriarch in Nicaea in 1219 and obtained his agreement to the separation of the Serbian church from the archbishopric in Ohrid. As archbishop, with his seat in the monastery of Žiča, he became the head of the independent Serbian church organization, that was at first divided into eight bishoprics. The changeover to the eastern church did not prevent good relations with the Catholic population in the coastal cities. For the Serbian kings in later years gave the people many privileges which bound them to their empire.

The efforts of the two brothers produced that close partnership between state and church which typified Serbia in the Middle Ages. It found its artistic expression in the magnificent monasteries that were built and heavily endowed by the ruling family. The beautiful frescoes dating from 1209 in the church at Studenica where Stefan Nemanja and his own son Stefan, the First-crowned, were buried, are impressive examples of Serbian monumental painting of the Raška School, which reached its greatest achievements in the thirteenth century with Mileševo (c. 1235), Peć (the church of the Holy Apostles, 1250), Morača (1252), and Sopočani (c. 1260). The religious foundations established by the Nemanjas and the Serbian aristocracy such as Dečani and Gračanica on the Kosovo Polje (the Field of the Blackbirds) (1321) are testimonies to the peak period of monastic life in the fourteenth and fifteenth centuries, just as are the works of the so-called 'Morava School' in the Morava plain at Ravanica (c. 1375), Lazarica (in Kruševac), Kalenić Ljubostinja and Manasija. Their ideas found expression in the proud series of 'lives' of Serbian rulers and church leaders that are among the most important Serbian literary creations of the Middle Ages. In Sava's and his brother Stefan's biography of Stefan Nemanja, written in their own hand, they bequeathed not merely a lasting monument to their father but also an influential ideological basis for the political achievements of the Nemanja dynasty.

Undoubtedly, their policies were only made possible by their favourable position on the edge of an area where conflicts between the powers were being fought out. With the withdrawal in 1204 of the Byzantine empire from the struggle for domination of the Balkan interior, the various newly-formed states were to concentrate their energies on controlling the Dardanelles and capturing the imperial city on the Bosphorus. Serbia remained largely unmolested and was able to survive a period of internal weakness.

But the policy pursued by Kalojan of Bulgaria of allowing himself to be drawn into competition with the Latin empire for the succession to the Byzantine domination, on the one hand, and with the world of the small feudal states of the Frankish lords and knights and the remnants of the Greek empire in Epirus and Asia Minor (Nicaea), on the other, was to prove fatal. Kalojan's initial successes seemed to justify his policy, and on April 14th, 1205, together with the Greek aristocracy resident in Thrace, he struck a decisive blow against the Latin empire of Baldwin of Flanders at Adrianople. However, he did not reap the fruits of this overwhelming victory, for in 1207 he died mysteriously – probably at the hand of a murderer – during his siege of Salonica, the capital of the kingdom of Boniface of Montferrat who had fallen in battle against the Bulgarians shortly before.

Boril (1207–1218), who usurped the Bulgarian throne at Trnovo, failed to cope with the growing internal and external problems, and the stability of his kingdom was particularly weakened by the desertion of powerful local rulers. Thus Slav, a nephew of Boril, tried to create an independent principality around his castle, Melnik, in the Rhodope mountains. The attempt failed but another such attempt was later made by the Vojvode Dobromit Chrysos who aimed to build up a kingdom between the two fronts around the impregnable rock-built castle at Prosek on the Vardar. Boril's inability to handle the Latins – he was defeated by the emperor Henry of Flanders at Philippopolis on July 31st, 1208 – on top of social and religious unrest characterized by the Synod of Trnovo of 1211, an unsuccessful attempt to control the

Bogomil movement, eventually compelled him to give up the throne to the legitimate heir, Ivan Asen II (1218–1241), whose reign marked the end of Bulgaria's period as a great power in the Middle Ages.

To begin with, Ivan Asen had formidable rivals in the Greek lords of Epirus, Michael Angelus and, after 1215, his half-brother, Theodore Angelus, who lived in Arta and then Yannina and temporarily enlarged their sphere of influence along the Adriatic coast to the region of Scutari to the north, and as far as Ohrid, Prilep and the river Maritsa to the east. Salonica fell to them in 1224. The Greek empire, which had become extinct, had seemed to rise once more with the coronation of Theodore Angelus in what had once been the second most powerful city of the Byzantine empire. The fall of Salonica, now an outpost of the Latin empire, together with Thessaly and parts of Macedonia, had given Theodore access to the Aegean. Taking advantage of this position, he turned towards Thrace in a last effort to become heir to the Byzantine empire. That had inevitably brought him into conflict with Ivan Asen, who had the very same designs on Greece and also had the diplomatic support of the Latin empire in Constantinople. The crushing defeat of Theodore Angelus, 'Basileus and Autokrator of the Romans', at Klokotnitsa on the river Maritsa in 1230 put an end to the ambitious designs of the despotate of Epirus. The Bulgarian tsar took over control of the central and western Balkans and extended his rule to Macedonia and part of Albania. His empire was to include Braničevo and Belgrade in the north as well as Adrianople in the east and Dyrrhachium (Durazzo) on the Adriatic, and he was able to influence the succession to the throne in Serbia, too. Undisputed supremacy for Bulgaria seemed to be within reach.

Ivan Asen turned Trnovo into a fine city, building beautiful palaces, churches and monasteries. The unpopular subordination of the Bulgarian church to Rome was brought to an end in 1235, and in agreement with the Orthodox church authorities a national Bulgarian church, with a Bulgarian patriarch at Trnovo, was established. But for Ivan Asen, as for his great tenth-century predecessor Simeon, the symbolic fulfilment of his claim to imperial rule–an entry into Constantinople–was never achieved. Even the close temporary alliance with John III Vatatzes of Nicaea (1222–1254), strengthened by the marriage in 1235 of his daughter to the emperor's son, Theodore Lascaris, did not bring him any closer to his objectives.

Bulgarian supremacy lasted but a short time after his death in 1241. For the Mongols stormed across eastern Europe in 1241/42 and completely changed the balance of power in the Danube region which received the brunt of their attack. Large parts of the Hungarian empire were devastated; the military power of Bulgaria was decisively weakened. It never fully recovered from this unexpected visitation. A decade later, in 1257, the dynasty of the Asenids died out, leaving a legacy of endless civil wars and struggles for power by individual claimants to the throne. The empire of Ivan Asen II had broken up into areas of local rule with strong separatist tendencies.

As a result, there was no serious opposition in the middle of the century to the rise of Serbia in the central Balkans and to the restoration of the Paleologi from Nicaea. In the 1240s, Bulgaria had lost her conquests in the border areas as John III Vatatzes had pushed forward the frontier of the Nicaean empire in Thrace to the Maritsa, and in Macedonia to the Vardar. Theodore Angelus, the despot of Epirus, who had been defeated at Klokotnitsa in 1230, and his son John had had to abandon their last stronghold in Salonica. At the same time, the empire built up by Michael II Angelus in Epirus and Thessaly from the wreckage of the western Greek empire had suffered great losses in western Macedonia, including the cities of Prilep and Ohrid. The Nicaean empire, now firmly established under Theodore II Lascaris (1254–1258), was to withstand the final onslaughts from the west that began when the son of the emperor Frederick II, Manfred of Sicily, adopting the old eastern policy of the Normans, formed an alliance in 1258 with Michael of Epirus and William Villehardouin of Achaea. The Serbian king, Stefan Uroš I (1243–1276), had joined in the alliance. The brilliant victory in 1259 of the 'Sevastokrator', John Paleologus, was to pave the way to Constantinople and on July 12th, 1261, its gates were drawn back for the entry

of the commander of the imperial army, Alexius Stratego-
poulus.

Two important events marked this last phase in the struggle for
Constantinople. In 1258, Manfred of Sicily had marched into the
Balkans occupying Corfu and the coastal towns facing it; and
Michael II of Epirus, in an affort to cement the alliance against the
Nicaean empire, had given his daughter Helen in marriage to
Manfred, and in the way of a dowry had presented his son-in-law
with the important coastal towns of Durazzo and Valona in 1259.
Charles of Anjou, Manfred's successor as king of Naples, was to
confirm his ownership of them after landing troops there in 1272.
He was only stopped from forming a new military alliance against
Byzantium of Epirots, Serbs, Bulgars, Albanians and the Venetian
navy by the 'Sicilian Vespers' of 1282, a matter that Peter III of
Aragon and Byzantine diplomacy had brought to a head. When
Charles Robert of Naples, whose grandfather Charles the Lame
had married Maria of Hungary, inherited the Hungarian throne
in 1308, the Angevins temporarily retained the Albanian coast
around Durazzo as the inheritance of the second in line. Later on,
however, in 1368, the region declared itself independent under a
local 'princeps Albaniae', Charles Thopia (d. 1388). His son,
George Thopia, handed it over to the Venetians and they held it
against the Ottomans until 1501.

Another significant event in the eastern Mediterranean was the
military alliance formed between the Italian maritime republic of
Genoa and the Nicaean empire by the treaty of Nymphaion of
March 13th, 1261. In return for being the most favoured nation,
Genoa, as counter-weight to Venice, was to collaborate with the
residual Byzantine empire of the Paleologi (1261–1453). So that
the competition between the two maritime powers was sharpened.
In the last two centuries of its survival, though, Byzantium was no
longer a serious rival to Venice. The emperor had been forced to
give up any attempt to rebuild the Byzantine navy, and the
Venetian republic was free to exercise its influence and interests in
the Adriatic and extend its power overseas.

The territorial gains of the newly created Byzantine empire made at the expense of the Bulgarian empire–now dissolved–and of what remained of the western Greek state around Epirus proved difficult to consolidate. In spite of a number of early successes, the dynasty of the Paleologi was unable to win back the commanding position Byzantium had once held in the central Balkan regions. This went instead to the struggling Serbian rulers for whom the Tatar invasion of 1241/42 had been welcome in that it had removed the pressure on their northern and western frontiers with Hungary and Bulgaria, and had opened up the possibility of a coalition in the final battle for the possession of Constantinople. In 1282, Stefan Uroš II (1282–1321), who had driven his brother Stefan Dragutin (1276–1282) from the throne, was to capture northern Macedonia and Skopje, and four years later he extended his influence to Bosnia and as far as the Albanian Adriatic coast. Among the outstanding achievements of his long reign were the creation of an orderly administration, the systematic development of trade, and an increase in the economic power of his country. With the help of German miners (Saxons) called in from Hungary, there began a revival of the Balkan mining industry which found a ready market in the commercial centres of Italy. The laborious carrying trade between the coast and the interior was largely operated by caravans owned by rich industrial families from Ragusa, and to a lesser extent by the inhabitants of Trogir (Tragusium or Trau) and Spalato (Split) for trade with Bosnia, and by the inhabitants of Cattaro and Antivari for that with Serbia. They also acted as enterprising financiers in the large-scale development of natural resources such as gold, silver, lead, copper and iron. They laid the foundations for the amazing rise of Serbian power in the fourteenth century, and gave Bosnia the backing it needed in the special position it held between Hungary and Serbia. It was within a short space of time that flourishing mining settlements and trading centres were established in the Balkan interior, and especially around the Kopaonik, which is so rich in minerals. Brskovo, Rudnik, Trepča and Rogozno were some of them, the most important mining town being Novo Brdo (Novus Mons, Novomonte or Nyenberghe) near Priština on the eastern edge of Kosovo Polje. (See also pages 25, 84 and 99.)

At this point, Bulgaria was once more in the ascendant in the power struggle, under the despot of Vidin, Michael (1324–1330), founder of the Šišmanid dynasty. Byzantium, where Andronicus III (1328–1341) had only recently managed to get control after years of civil war, was being menaced in Asia Minor by the rapid advance of the Turks, and Brussa (Bursa) had fallen in 1326. Neither of these countries was prepared to accept the rise of Serbia without challenge. The threatened banding together of Byzantine and Bulgarian military contingents was forestalled by Stefan Uroš III Dečanski (1322–1331) who annihilated the Bulgarian forces at the decisive battle of Velbužd (Küstendil) on July 28th, 1330. Tsar Michael III Šišman fell in the battle. With his death the Bulgarian empire was again to go into decline and less than two generations later it was finally conquered by Ottoman armies. King Uroš III was to be cheated of the rewards of his victory. For the energetic and popular prince, Stefan Dušan, his co-ruler, whose brave personal intervention was decisive in the winning of the victory at Velbužd, was supported by a growing faction in the Serbian nobility, and this gave him the opportunity to seize the highest office. A few months after, the deposed king lost his life during an attempt to escape from prison.

In a remarkable triumphal campaign the young king Stefan Dušan Uroš IV (1331–1355) now built up a Serbian empire that embraced the Dalmatian coast and the main cities of Albania– where only Durazzo remained in the hands of the Angevins– Epirus, Macedonia (including Ohrid, Prilep, Kastoria, Strumica and Vodena, Salonica alone remaining in Byzantine hands), parts of central Greece, and, to the north, the strategically important Morava-Vardar area that included Belgrade. He even ventured into Bulgaria. The state of virtual civil war in the Byzantine empire caused by the attempt of John VI Cantacuzenus (emperor 1347–1354) to usurp the throne, the socio-revolutionary movement of the Zelots in Salonica after 1342, and religious strife in the form of Palamism and Hesychasm were to paralyse any efforts to resist the advance of the Serbs in the Balkans and the attacks of the Turks in Asia Minor. After his magnificent coronation by the Serbian patriarch as 'Emperor of the Serbs and Greeks' on April

16th, 1346, in Ohrid, Stefan Dušan set himself the same political target as other Balkan rulers had done in the past: the re-creation of an all-embracing Balkan empire centred on Constantinople. His ambitious plans, too, were thwarted by the impregnable walls of the city.

Of more permanent value were his attempts to strengthen his empire internally. It had been undergoing extensive hellenization since it had moved from the area of the original Serbian settlement towards the south, to Prizren, Prilep and Ohrid, which were under Greek influence. In questions of court ceremony, the running of the chancery and government administration, he was to follow the Byzantine example. The famous legal code of tsar Dušan, the 'Zakonik', helped the process of codification. It was approved in May 1349 by an assembly of the nobility in Skopje, and in 1354 had been extended and completed in Seres (Serrai). The code was an attempt to combine inherited traditional law with the Byzantine code.

It was the feudal nobility rather than the imperial central power who really benefited from Stefan Dušan's Serbian 'grand design'. Not only did they enjoy the spoils of war and the all-round increase in trade and industry but they also moved into the new administrative posts and into influential positions at court which, combined with their widespread ownership of the land, gave them positions of power that could be further developed. And so it was that, after the sudden death of the tsar on December 20th, 1355, hopes for a centralized Serbian state were dashed by the personal interests of the nobility. The Serbo-Greek empire was to dissolve into a number of territorial units governed by powerful princely dynasties. The young tsar Stefan Uroš V (1355–1371) held but nominal supremacy, and even this was contested by his uncle Simeon, the half-brother of Stefan Dušan, as ruler of Epirus, Thessaly and Aetolia, who had himself crowned king of the Serbs and Greeks at Trikkala.

Again, different parts of the country followed their own separate paths of development. In the Albanian area, local leaders formed independent domains; there was Andreas Muzaka, and there was also Charles Thopia, who took Durazzo from the Angevins; in

Valona and Kanina, a Bulgar named Ivan Asen established himself. In Macedonia, the brothers Mrnjavčevići rose to leadership, Vukašin ruling as 'King of the Serbs and Greeks' from 1365 on in the areas around Prilep, Skopje and Prizren, and his brother Uglješ in the area of Seres. In southern Macedonia, Bogdan maintained his position at Jug Bogdan and the Dejanovići in Kumanovo, Velbužd, Štip and Strumica, while Vuk Branković controlled the region round Kosovo. The centrifugal tendencies extended into the old Serbian countryside, too: in the Zeta the Balšići brothers–Stracimir, Georg and Balsa Balšić–created an independent position for themselves; in Herzegovina, Vojislav Vojnović did the same, but then had to give way to his nephew, Nikola Altomanović; the prince of Morava-Serbia was Lazar I Hrebeljanović.

Similar manifestations of disintegration characterized the political life of the Bulgarians in the last phase before the Ottoman conquest. The Black Sea coastal areas round Varna were subordinated to Balsić and his brother, the despot Dobrotić (after whom the Dobrudja was probably named), and the Hungarians advanced from the north, increasing their sphere of influence. Implacable enmity among the members of the ruling family of the Šišmanids had made it impossible for them to think of organizing any defence. John the Elder (Ivan) Stracimir, who had at first come to terms with Vidin but later went over as vassal to the Hungarian side, had quarrelled bitterly with his step-brother, Ivan Šišman (1371–1393), and had driven him, in his sixties, over to the side of the Turkish sultan. The land, torn by internal strife, was become an easy prey for the Ottomans.

A flourishing cultural life was the sole redeeming feature in the declining years of mediaeval Bulgaria. Hesychasm, which had come from Byzantium to Trnovo, was to give rise to an unprecedented revival of literature among the circle of the last Bulgarian patriarch, Euthymius (1373–1393). He gathered a 'school' around him, and his reform of the written language had influence far beyond Bulgarian frontiers–especially in the eastern Slavonic regions. His lives of the saints, among them St. Ivan of the monastery of Rila, established a tradition in this type of literature.

The inevitable break-up of the central Balkan territories into an impotent world of small states allowed the political emergence of areas on the upper Bosna that had for long lived in the shadow of powerful neighbours. During the tenth century the Serbians under prince Časlav and the Croatians under king Krešimir had taken turns in ruling Bosnia; later, after a short period under the Byzantine empire of Basil II, the country had been drawn into the orbit of the Serbian princes of Dioclea. During his campaign to acquire Serbian territories, Constantine Bodin had brought Bosnia under his control, and he appointed prince Stefan governor. The Hungarian expansion towards Croatia and Dalmatia had been accompanied by a growth in Hungarian influence and had placed these countries in a position of dependence; and since 1138, the Hungarian kings had laid claim in their royal title to Bosnia. The title 'Ban', attested for the first time in the twelfth century as a designation for the Bosnian rulers, was borrowed from the Hungarians, and by them from the Avars.

It was its religious characteristics that gave medieval Bosnia its special individuality. Situated as it was on the demarcation line between the spheres of influence of the western and eastern churches, Bosnia in the twelfth century had built up an independent 'Bosnian church' organization of 'heretical' character. This had been achieved between 1180 and 1204 under Ban Kulin who had publicized the heretical teachings of the Bogomils–brought across from Bulgaria to take root in Bosnia in defiance of all papal representations and counter-measures. At the head of the 'Bosnian church' stood the *djed*, and under him in hierarchical ranking came the *gosti* and the *starci*. The church could count on the good will of the aristocracy since common interests bound the two closely together. The church was against Rome and against Hungarian attempts at reconversion to Catholicism, while the aristocracy was against outside intervention and the strengthening of the central power. In face of this alliance of common aims, the crusade against Bosnia of 1234–1239 initiated by the pope and led by the Hungarian king Andreas II (1205–1235) and his son, the Croatian Ban Koloman, was bound to fail. Inspired by a national will to resistance, Ban Mathias Ninoslav (1232–1250), whose political activities were not always easy to account for, reversed the early successes of the crusade.

The internal and external conditions necessary for bringing about political secession from neighbouring Hungary did not yet exist in the thirteenth century. So in 1254, the successors of Mathias Ninoslav had to give formal recognition to Hungarian supremacy, which meant the division of the country into administrative areas. The northern regions called the Banats of Usora and Soli, were separated from upper Bosnia and Dolnji-Kraji, and the north-eastern part was joined to the Banat of Mačva–between the Drina, Sava, Danube and Morava. The overlordship of these areas was entrusted to close relatives of the Hungarian ruling house in the next decades. In the years between 1282 and 1314, Mačva-Bosnia was in the hands of the one-time Serbian king Stefan Dragutin, a brother-in-law of the Hungarian king Ladislas IV. The weakness of the Hungarian central authority during the wars of succession after the death of Ladislas in 1290 was to encourage the rise of local chieftains. And in Bosnia the Croatian noble family of Šubić temporarily gained an independent position of power in 1299 to 1322. According to the records, the Ban Paul Šubić held the proud title of 'Ban of Croatia and Dalmatia and Lord of Bosnia'. Mladen Šubić (1302–1322) was eventually deposed from his position in Croatia and Bosnia by a conspiracy of local noblemen who, in agreement with the Hungarian king Charles Robert, brought his ward Stefan II Kotromanić (1322–1353) to power.

Under Stefan Kotromanić began the real rise to power of mediaeval Bosnia, for he acquired the land of Hum which till then had been under Serbian rule–it was Zahumlje, better known after the chief Vojvode Stefan Vukčić had had the title of duke bestowed on him in the year 1448 as 'the land of the Duke', i.e. Herzegovina–and with the addition of the coastal strip between Ragusa and Almissa (Omiš) in the Cetina estuary he secured access on a wide front to the Adriatic. The finances for this expensive foreign policy came, as also in neighbouring Serbia, from the rich mineral resources that had been opened up with the help of Saxon miners, Srebrnica, Olovo, Kreševo and Fojnica being among the new mining towns. There was no reason for him to expect any insuperable difficulties. Stefan Dušan of Serbia's policy was directed towards the regions under Greek influence in the south, and Hungary was dependent on military assistance from Bosnia both in Croatia and in its quarrels with its Venetian rival. So that Stefan Kotromanić's nephew and successor, Ban Tvrtko I (1353–1391), had nothing to fear from his Serbian neighbour nor from his Hungarian overlord, either. After Stefan Dušan's death, an alliance with the Serbian prince Lazar against Nikola Altomanović brought with it a further acquisition of territory on the upper Drina and in Travunia (Trebinje). Furthermore, the death of Louis I of Hungary in 1382 led to the restitution and extension of territories on the Dalmatian coast as far as Ragusa, including Cattaro in 1385. As early as 1377, Tvrtko had himself crowned at the tomb of St. Sava in Mileševo as king of Serbia, Bosnia and the coastal regions. He was able to justify his pretensions to the Serbian throne by his family connections with the house of Nemanja. And in 1390, he added claims to Croatia and Dalmatia in his title. His death in 1391 cut short the work he was doing to bring about the political unification of the Croatian and Serbian races; but in fact, the internal will to survive had now vanished in face of the new external situation. The unchecked drive of the Ottoman empire to conquer the Balkans was restricting the activity of the princes. In 1393, the Hungarian kingdom in the north brought the border regions of Bosnia, that is, Croatia and Dalmatia, back under its influence. The incompetence of Tvrtko's successors and the undisguised self-interest of the powerful ruling class had contributed to the decline. It was only by virtue of its favourable situation between the Turkish and Hungarian powers that the total decline of Bosnia was postponed for nearly a century–till 1463.

The dissolution of the Serbian empire after the death of Stefan Dušan in 1355 started a movement of peoples that was to be of great significance in Balkan history: it was the movement of Albanian settlers to the south through Epirus, through the north-western regions of Acarnania and Aetolia, and then in a broad stream into central Greece, including Boeotia and Attica, and as far as the

85

Peloponnese. The Albanian and 'Wallachian' wandering shepherds, descendants of those Balkan-Roman elements of the population who had fled to the mountain areas before the advance of the Slavs, had already been on the move in previous centuries, and some of them had adopted a settled way of life. During the eleventh and twelfth centuries, Albanians had moved down from the mountains to the coastal lowlands of lower Albania, and in the thirteenth century they had attacked western Macedonia and the region of Epirus. Of the indigenous leaders who achieved political power after 1355, the family of Charles Thopia (1359–1388) won a dominant position in the area between Durazzo, Kruja and Antivari (Bar), as I have mentioned, and the Balšići (the Balsha family) to the north and east of Scutari. The bitter struggles between these families in which, the Turks began to take sides— first of all as allies of the Thopia family in 1385–gave other families the chance to achieve power and recognition. Among them were the Dukagjini, the Shiptas, the Muzaka, the Arianites and the Castriotes. It was in the defensive campaigns against the invading Ottomans that one of the members of the Castriote family, owner of many estates around Kruja, gave the Albanians a decisive impulse towards political unification. He and another remarkable hero in the struggle for independence, John Hunyadi, were the only bright stars in this darkest period of Balkan political history. (See pages 91–2 and 95–6.)

The political future of the 'Wallachian' shepherds, however, lay beyond the Danube in Transylvania and the principalities of Moldavia and Wallachia, though they frequently exercised their influence on central Balkan affairs, and the participation of Vlachs and Cumans had helped the brothers Peter and Asen to achieve success in their uprising of 1185 when the Second Bulgarian Empire was founded. Traces of Wallachian settlers can still be found today in Albania and Epirus (the Pindus), west Macedonia and the hinterland of Salonica in the shape of the Kutzo-, Macedo-, or Mauro-Wallachians, i.e. the 'Black Wallachians', and the Morlaks and Cincars.

6

THE OTTOMAN CONQUEST AND THE DECLINE OF THE BALKAN STATES IN THE FOURTEENTH CENTURY

The Balkan states of the fourteenth century fell quickly in turn to the Ottoman conquerors who faced no united defence after their first victory on the European mainland at Gallipoli in 1354. Within a few score years a new overall political organization had been imposed from outside on the Balkan peoples; separatist tendencies and interests had once more been forced into an imperial framework. The various attempts on the part of local princes through the centuries to make their own areas of sovereignty the rallying points for general movements for the unification of the Balkan peoples had never got beyond promising starts. There had been the efforts to establish a Greco-Slav state of Simeon of Bulgaria in the tenth century, of his successor Samuel, and of Ivan Asen II, too, and later still those of Stefan Dušan and Tvrtko of Bosnia. Even the most energetic Byzantine rulers like Basil II, the Comneni emperors and Michael VIII Paleologus had failed to restore a Byzantine empire stretching east and west from one sea to another and to the north as far as the Danube, the Roman frontier. It was under the Turkish crescent that the Balkan peninsula again found political unity.

The Ottoman conquest was not unexpected. The devastating defeat of the Byzantines at Manzikert in 1071, which had cleared the way into Asia Minor for the Seljuks, had made clear the danger of the rapidly developing Turkish principalities in the east. Then the rise of the Ottoman dynasty at the beginning of the fourteenth century quickly produced a new, immediate military threat. It came from the military élite of defenders of the Faith, the Gazi, who, battling against Byzantium and the Christian Crusader countries on the soil of Asia Minor, had shown themselves capable of achievements involving greater statesmanship.

From their seat at Bursa (Brussa), the Ottoman rulers began by uniting the numerous Turkish feudal domains in Asia Minor into an organized political entity. In 1353, they finally ventured onto the European mainland, where they had become thoroughly familiar with conditions after their participation in the Byzantine civil war. There had been a treaty between John Cantacuzenus and Orchan in 1345. As early as 1365, sultan Murad I (1359–1389) was able to transfer his capital from Bursa to Adrianople, which had fallen into Ottoman hands in 1362. The first city governor to represent the sultan in the European part of the empire, Lala Šahin, settled in Philippopolis (Plovdiv). He carried the title of 'Beglerbeg' of Rumelia, that is, of Byzantium since the official name for a Byzantine was 'Rhoman'. In the following decades the sultan's generals conquered the remaining states and local principalities in the Balkans, and eventually stormed the walls of Constantinople in 1453.

The success of this grandiose work of conquest was due not only to the irresistible strength of the Ottoman armies and their superiority in the art of war but also to a complete lack of co-operation among the Christian princes. Attempts on the part of papal diplomacy and the more judicious potentates to give assistance to the declining Balkan Christian states from the west had always ended in miserable failure, especially since they mostly involved unrealistic demands for union with the Roman Church. That had, for example, been the case with the expedition of count Amadeus VI of Savoy, 'il Conte Verde', a relative of the Byzantine ruling family; with the enterprise of the 'Crusaders' at Nicopolis in 1396; and with the final attempt to bring succour under the leadership of John Hunyadi and the youthful Polish-Hungarian king Ladislas III that had led to the catastrophe of Varna in 1444.

Local strongpoints were destroyed by the Ottoman troops, often after grim battles. Of the Serbian princes, fate first overtook the brothers John Ugljes and 'king' Vukašin. They had raised a considerable army and had been hoping to repel the advancing Ottomans and contain them in Macedonia, which was under their control. On September 26th, 1371, they together suffered a crushing defeat at Černomen on the river Maritsa. Neither of them survived, and Macedonia fell to the victors. The Dejanović brothers and Vukašin's son Kraljević Marko, the 'king's son', whose memory is preserved in a Serbian cycle of heroic ballads, had to participate in later campaigns as Turkish vassals; and in 1395, Marko and Constantine Dejanović fell in battle against Mircea the Old's 'Vlachs' (Wallachians) near Rovine, north of the Danube.

In the year of the defeat at Černomen and the extinction of the Serbian Nemanjić dynasty through the death of Stefan Uroš V (1355–1371), a chance was given to the Serbian prince Lazar to change the course of destiny from his base in Morava-Serbia and Raška. Good relations with his up-and-coming Bosnian neighbour Tvrtko had brought him considerable territorial gains at the expense of Nikola Altomanović. A clever matrimonial policy had secured him powerful allies such as Vuk Branković in the Priština region and George II Balšić of Zeta. Turkish successes in Albania, greatly aided by Charles Thopia's request for help against his rivals in the Balšići family in 1385, and also in Bulgaria—culminating in the capture of Sofia in 1382 and Niš in 1386—threatened to produce a dangerous scissor movement against the allies. So prince Lazar had to agree to pay tribute like the Bulgarian tsar Ivan Šišman at Trnovo before him. Then in 1387, a combined effort of Serbs, Bosnians and Bulgarians led to an overwhelming victory over an Ottoman army division under the command of Lala Šahin at Pločnik on the Toplica. The Turkish advance into Bosnia ended in a similar failure. However, these episodes were not decisive. Both sides now mobilized for a final assault. A Turkish campaign in eastern Bulgaria forced Ivan Šišman, who had broken away and become independent, to accept Turkish domination once again, and secured that flank for further operations against the Serbs. On June 15th, 1389, the famous *Vidovan* (St. Vitus' day), prince Lazar together with Vuk Branković and their Bosnian allies under the leadership of the Vojvode Vlatko Vuković, supported by Croatian, Albanian, Bulgarian and Wallachian troops, challenged the sultan Murad on the Kosovo Polje.

The killing of the sultan during the ensuing battle by the legendary Serb, Miloš Obilić, gave the encounter a dramatic character. The Serbs' violent attack confused the Turks and for a time their position was critical, but the determination of Bayazit, the successor to the throne, brought about another victory for the Turks in spite of their severe losses. The ageing prince Lazar and his immediate followers were taken prisoner and executed. Vuk Branković's alleged betrayal belongs to the fund of legends which this bloody battle inspired, and which embroidered with high drama the collapse of the Serbian army and its aristocratic leaders. Though prince Stefan Lazarević (1389–1427) was at first to be a Turkish vassal, he was able during the Turkish wars of succession at the beginning of the fifteenth century to establish himself in a position of power near Belgrade and Mačva as an ally of king Sigismund of Hungary.

Sultan Bayazit Yildirim, the 'lightning' (1389–1402), devoted the following years to completing his father's task of conquering the Balkans. A terrible fate befell the city of Trnovo, the ancient city of the Bulgarian tsars, which was taken by storm in the year 1393. The patriarch Euthymius was exiled to Macedonia and a large section of the population was resettled in Asia Minor. The Turkish sword next reached beyond the frontiers of the Danube and, after the inconclusive battle on the field of Rovine of May 17th, 1395, forced the courageous Wallachian prince Mircea the Old into a position of semi-dependence. The Hungarian king tried to divert the imminent danger from himself by taking his army down the Danube, having recruited western, and especially French, knights to strengthen it. To begin with, his successes gave him cause for hope. The Bulgarian ruler of Vidin, tsar Stracimir, defeated its Turkish garrison and after some resistance opened the city's gates. But on September 25th, 1396, the sultan, who had arrived in haste from Trnovo, inflicted a crushing defeat on the Christian knights at Nicopolis, and what was left of Bulgarian territory around Vidin lost its independence. By the end of the fourteenth century, Bulgaria right up to the Danube was firmly in Turkish hands.

The unexpected defeat and capture of sultan Bayazit by the

Mongolian world conqueror, Timur Lenk or Tamerlane, at the battle of Ankara in 1402, brought but temporary relief to the Balkan peoples. For they did not know how to take advantage of the opportunity they had been given. Mehmed I (1413–1421) together with his brothers Suleiman and Musa put a final end to the bloody wars of succession at the decisive battle of Čamorlu near Philippopolis, where the Serbian vassals–and George Branković in particular–earned themselves lasting fame. He thus enabled his successor, sultan Murad II (1421–1451), to continue a forward policy in the Balkans. In 1422, Constantinople had to withstand a siege, and in 1430, Salonica, which had only come under Venetian domination in 1423, fell prey to the Ottoman conquerors.

The Hungarian-Turkish conflict was now to overshadow all further Balkan developments. A large part of Serbian territory was already under Turkish rule. But in the north, near Hungary, an independent area had survived around Smederevo (Semendria). Over this a fierce struggle took place. Though the sultan succeeded in taking Smederevo in 1439, his siege of Belgrade in the following year was unsuccessful. In this situation the hopes of Christendom rested with a glorious war hero who had been victorious in several clashes with Turkish armies and was in time to lead a motley army of Crusaders across the Danube under the command of the Jagellonian king of Poland and Hungary, Ladislas III. He was John Hunyadi, duke of Transylvania, the 'Sibinjanin Janko' of Serbian folk songs. His army advanced via Kruševac, Niš and Pirot to Sofia, and won a brilliant victory at Jalovac on the way to Philippopolis. During its retreat, another victory was gained in a rearguard action at Kunovica (1443).

In view of the precarious position of his empire because of internal difficulties in Asia Minor and the Albanian uprising of 'Skanderbeg', Murad II proposed a ten-year truce and the restitution to the Serbian despot, George Branković, of his territory around Smederevo. At the meeting of the assembly in Szegedin in 1444, oaths of agreement were sworn. However, they were only to last a few months. At the instigation of the papal envoy, cardinal Julian Cesarini, Ladislas and John Hunyadi were persuaded to undertake another military expedition. Insufficient preparation and a lack of firm co-ordination with their allies brought that surprising adventure to a humiliating end before Varna on November 10th, 1444. King Ladislas and cardinal Cesarini met with their deaths. John Hunyadi was not to concede defeat until 1448 after another battle on the Kosovo Polje.

It was George Branković who saved what remained of Serbian independence. By clever policy, he succeeded in maintaining his position in the zone between the Hungarian and Turkish areas of sovereignty for many years. His capital was Smederevo, and he controlled the areas around Golubac, Kruševac and Novo Brdo. In 1456, he withstood a Turkish attack on Smederevo and Belgrade, which John Hunyadi and the papal legate, John Capistramus, relieved on July 21st–22nd with a fine victory. Three years later, though, the Serbian despotate had ceased to exist. For to the horror of western civilization, sultan Mehmed II, Fatih, the 'Conqueror' (1451–1481), entered Smederevo without a fight in 1459. The road to Hungary lay wide open.

During the reign of the great conqueror Mehmed II all remaining local resistance in the Balkans was crushed. In 1453, the Christian world learnt with sympathy and dismay of the fall on May 29th of the proud metropolis on the Bosphorus, which for decades had suffered the concentrated attacks of the Ottoman empire from land and sea. The famous cathedral of St. Sophia, the symbol of the Orthodox world, was turned into a mosque. The remaining Greek areas survived but a few years, Mistra in the Peloponnese being conquered in 1460, and the empire of Trebizond on the Black Sea in 1461.

Equally important for the consolidation of Ottoman power was the final subjugation of the Slav and Albanian races in the western and north-western Balkans. In 1463, the last Bosnian king, Stefan Tomašević (1461–1463), saw his realm overcome in a surprise Turkish attack. In spite of a radical change in his religious policy by which the Bosnian church had been renounced in favour of Roman Catholicism, he had waited in vain for help from the west. In earlier decades the Bosnian aristocracy, among them Hrvoje Vukčić-Hrvatinić, Sandalj Hranić Kosača and the Pavlovići, had embarked on a dangerous course by playing off the Turks against

Map 7. The Ottoman empire in the late fifteenth century

Hungary. When Vukčić-Hrvatinić summoned the enemy into his country, it was no longer possible to halt the decline. The Bogomils' dislike of the Catholic Croats and Hungarians as well as the Orthodox Serbs had long become a nation-wide characteristic, and it helped prepare the ground for the conversion of most of Bosnia to Islam under Turkish rule. By such mass conversion, the Bosnian aristocracy was able to retain its land ownership and privileged social position in the centuries that followed. Later immigration of Orthodox Serbs who had avoided Ottoman pressure was to make Bosnia one of the most heterogeneous territories of south-eastern Europe: there, in a small area, both the eastern and western churches existed side by side with Islam.

The decline of Bosnia put an end to the separate development of the regions to the south, too, which under the Vojvode Sandalj Hranić Kosača and Stefan Vukčić Kosača (1435–1466) had become independent and gained a great deal by their good relations with the Turks. As a base for operations against Bosnia, the area had come under direct Ottoman rule. Their last city on the Adriatic coast fell in 1482.

Matthias Corvinus, the son of the victor over the Turks, John Hunyadi, was only able as king of Hungary to control for a time the northern border areas of Serbia and Bosnia–Dolnji-Kraji and Usora–which were included in the Banats of Srebrenica and Jajce. For they were annexed by the Turks at the beginning of the sixteenth century in 1512 and 1522, along with Belgrade in 1521 and, after the defeat in 1526 of the young Jagellon, Louis II, at Mohács, the greater part of the kingdom of Hungary. The collaboration of the Vojvode of Transylvania, John Zápolya, with sultan Suleiman II brought the Turks to the gates of Vienna in 1529, though it was without success that they besieged it from September 29th to October 15th of that year. The Habsburgs, who, as a result of the treaty of succession of 1515, had followed the Jagellons on the throne of St. Stephen, thus found themselves restricted to the northern and north-western border areas of Hungary. While the Croats approved the succession of the Habsburgs at the assembly held at Cetina in 1527, the Hungarian magnates supported John Zapolya. With the backing of the sultan,

Zapolya retained a special position as leader of a Magyar nationalist party until his death in 1543. After that, the Turkish crescent was to fly over the Hungarian capital, Ofen, for over a hundred and fifty years. It was not until the progressive collapse of the Ottoman empire after the second siege of Vienna in 1683 that the Habsburgs were gradually able to take over their inheritance in Hungary.

With the support of the Venetian navy in their rear, the Adriatic coastal areas of the Balkan peninsula were more successful in resisting the Turkish conquerors. In the hills of Montenegro and Albania, the advancing Turkish armies met with bitter guerilla warfare and suffered many severe rebuffs, and George Castriota 'Skanderbeg', who had been brought up at the court of the sultan, organized a national rising among the Albanian peoples which western Christendom considered of great significance. In March 1444, he rallied the local princes at Alessio to form a close alliance of all leaders of nationalist forces, the 'Albanian League'. Against the overwhelmingly superior forces of the Turks he held his ground till he died – in 1468.

Due to the rivalries between noble families, Albanian territory had already been in danger of being divided up between the Turks and the Venetians at the end of the fourteenth century. In the family feud between the Balšići and the Thopia in 1385, the sultan had sided with the latter – not least at the battle of Vijosa – while the Venetians had secured for themselves the coastal towns including Durazzo and Scutari. However, the events leading to the battle of Kosovo Polje in 1389, the disaster for the Turks at the battle of Ankara against Tamerlane in 1402, and the quarrels within the Ottoman dynasty and ensuing feuds between brothers – together with Turkish entanglements on the Hungarian frontier – resulted in a temporary withdrawal of their troops. Only in the second decade of the fifteenth century did the Turks continue their policy of conquest by the occupation of important places in central Albania, as elsewhere: Kruja or Akce Hisar, 'the White Citadel', fell in 1415, Valona, Kanina and Berat in 1417, and Girokastra in 1419. Albania was to become a *sanjak* of the Ottoman empire (Sancak-i Arvanid; later Sancak-i Arnaud) in 1430, after the uprising during the Turkish-Venetian war of 1428 organized by the lord of Mati and Dibra, Ivan Castriota, had been quashed. Ivan remained on his estates as a Turkish vassal and sent three of his sons to the court of the sultan in Adrianople as hostages. One of them, George, the sultan entrusted with the government of Kruja in 1438; and in 1440 he entered Dibra as a 'Sanjak-beg'.

George Castriota (1405–1468), known as 'Skanderbeg', used this unusual position of trust to conspire against his overlord, as we have seen, and proceeded to enter into secret relations with the Italian sea-powers of Naples and Venice and the king of Hungary. In 1443, during the victorious advance of John Hunyadi, he openly led an insurrection, and in November he declared Albania independent at Kruja. As commander of the forces of the 'Albanian League', he destroyed a Turkish army under Ali Pasha in June 1444. In 1450, he successfully defended Kruja against a scissor movement by superior Turkish forces. Although he received no outside help, he held his ground in a bitter battle near Oranik in 1456, and finally he gained a remarkable surprise victory on September 7th, 1457, below Kruja. But because Skanderbeg was unable to organize a western crusade during his two periods of residence in Italy, the Albanian struggle for independence was denied ultimate success. He himself did not live to see the ending of Albanian freedom. He died on January 17th, 1468, and even after his death the Turks had great difficulty in breaking the resistance of Albanian strongholds supported by the Venetians. Alessio and Durazzo did not fall till 1501, and Ulcinj and Bar only in 1571. The Albanians were to retain the freedom of the hills for many years to come. As in Montenegro, the Turkish conquerors had to be satisfied with the control of strategically important places and areas accessible by road.

In the second half of the fifteenth century, Montenegro gained a temporary advantage through the dispute between Venice and Turkey. This provided the opportunity for the rise of the Crno-jevići family, who eventually exchanged her position of Venetian protectorate for that of Turkish vassal state, and developed their residence, Cetinje, into a cultural centre—where, among other things, the first Serbian printing press was set up. Montenegro was formally incorporated into the Ottoman empire in 1499.

The forced withdrawal of the Venetians from important outposts on Albanian territory was symptomatic of the new balance of power in south-eastern Europe at the turn of the sixteenth century. Since about 1000, the Venetian republic had been able to build up an expanding overseas empire in the Levant, the 'Oltramare', with the help of a powerful navy. The treaty of 1204 made by the Latin conquerors of Constantinople laid down a legal basis for the division of the Byzantine empire, three-eighths of Byzantine territory being ceded to the Venetians. However, in spite of limiting themselves to coastal areas, easily defensible territories and strategically important cities—e.g. Durazzo, Cephalonia, Zakinthos, Modon, Koron, Salonica, Negroponte (Euboea) and the Aegean islands—so as to protect the freedom of the seas, Venice suffered heavy losses during the thirteenth century. The government was able to retain its territories in Istria in its struggle against the political ambitions of the patriarchs of Aquileia; it also succeeded in suppressing the movement for independence of the republic of Zara (Zadar) in 1242–1243 organized by Hungary and the Ban Koloman. But a further advance on the part of Hungary towards the Adriatic coast could no longer be halted.

In 1357–58, a century later, Venetian supremacy in Dalmatia collapsed. By the peace treaty of February 18th, 1358, king Louis of Hungary extracted a far-reaching declaration of policy from the Venetians in which they renounced all claim to places such as Spalato (Split), Trav (Trogir), Sebenico (Šibenik), Nona (Nin), and Brazza (Brač) and agreed to evacuate them. It required an extreme effort on the part of Venice to emerge triumphant from a confrontation in 1378 with Hungary, Genoa and Padua, who had formed an alliance and had been joined by duke Albrecht III of Austria. By the peace treaty of Turin of 1381, she won back Chioggia; but Hungary was confirmed in her possession of the Dalmatian territories. Not until conquest by the Ottomans was threatened, were the Venetians able to regain some of their lost territories and some of the coastal cities. Under Turkish pressure, the Albanian families of the Balšići and the Thopia were to transfer

97

to the Venetians the ownership of places such as Valona, which had since 1388 been temporarily in Venetian hands; Durazzo, which was handed over by George Thopia in 1392 and remained in Venetian possession till 1501; Alessio, Scutari and Drivasto (1396); and finally, in the fifteenth century, Dulcigno (Ulcinj), Budua (Budva) and Antivari (Bar). Owing to the weakness of the Hungarian kingdom at the turn of the fifteenth century, Venice's dominating position in Venezia Giulia and the territories which she had lost in Dalmatia were restored. Zara was taken in 1409, and the other cities fell between 1419 and 1421.

Under these circumstances the Turks' advance towards the Adriatic coast (where they entered Valona in 1417) was bound to lead to a confrontation there with the Venetian navy. Venetian diplomacy anticipated the danger and tried, after some hesitation, to halt Turkish expansion with the assistance of local resistance movements. Venice's strength was also put to the test in the Aegean area where she repaired her defence establishments in the Peloponnese and on Euboea, and acquired Salonica by purchase in 1423. The outcome of the first eastern confrontation was in Venice's favour. On May 29th, 1416, at Gallipoli she had won a splendid naval victory, and her peace treaty with sultan Mehmed I (1413–1421) guaranteed her free trade. The settlement after the fall of Salonica to the Turks in 1430 once again recognized her possessions in the Aegean and on the Albanian coast.

As a result, however, of a number of small-scale military operations, Venice was progressively forced out of her positions in the east and on the Adriatic coast from the middle of the fifteenth century onwards. Armed conflicts continued over a period of sixteen years after 1463, during which Venetian seapower was much shaken by the rapid development of a Turkish navy. Negroponte fell into Turkish hands in 1470, and her distant outposts in the Black sea area, Kaffa among them, were lost in 1475. In 1474, Scutari was still able to withstand a siege, but on June 15th, 1478, Kruja, which had been so hotly contested, had to open its gates after a two-year investment. Alessio and Drivasto could not be defended, either. Then in 1479, Venice had to pay heavily for peace by renouncing Scutari and other important Albanian and

Dalmatian cities. Only Dulcigno (under Venice from 1423 to 1571), Antivari (1442–1571), Budua (1442–1797) and Durazzo (1392–1501) were saved from the general collapse. Not even the lucky capture of Cyprus in 1489 could delay her evident decline. During a later, second Turkish war, her fleet was conclusively defeated off Modon on August 20th, 1499. The following year saw the collapse of Venetian supremacy in the Peloponnese (in the Morea); and Lepanto, Modon, Koron, and Navarino had to be surrendered under the peace treaty of 1502–3. Durazzo had already fallen in 1501. The remaining islands of the Levantine empire were evacuated during the reigns of Suleiman II, 'the Magnificent' (1520–1566), and his successor, Selim II (1566–1574). Cyprus was lost in 1571. Crete alone survived – that is, until the twenty-five year war of 1645–1669. Neither the important though often over-estimated naval victory at Lepanto on October 7th, 1571, a day which the Catholic Church celebrates as the 'feast of the rosary', nor the successful counter-offensive of the 'Holy Alliance' of Habsburgs, Poles and Venetians after the relief of Vienna in 1683 helped the Venetians to restore their earlier position. In the Adriatic region, after the Napoleonic interlude, the succession went eventually to the Habsburgs.

In the collapse of the Venetian empire and the Balkan interior before the Turks, only the aristocratic republic of Ragusa (Dubrovnik) survived more or less unscathed. The former refugee settlement, established in the seventh century before the advance of the Avars and Slavs, had known how to compensate for the lack of a protective hinterland by making skilful alliances with neighbouring powers most likely to be of help, such as, for instance, Venice, Hungary, Serbia and Bosnia. After the decline of Byzantine influence, Ragusa was semi-dependent on Venice for a century and a half from 1205–1358, which helped her trade to flourish and developed her commercial connections: most trade within the Balkans and most links with the Italian coastal cities were kept up by her merchants; the coal mines in the Balkan interior offered opportunities for profitable capital investment. Ragusa had adopted an aristocratic constitution on Venetian lines which guaranteed a controlling influence to the wealthy city patricians. The city did not, however, reach its zenith until after the period of Hungarian-Croatian rule lasting from 1358–1526. This occurred in the time of Turkish supremacy when in return for tribute it received extensive trading rights within the Ottoman empire. After 1683, it was to win an increasingly independent position in the Adriatic.

In the palaces of Ragusa's wealthy bourgeoisie there were many patrons of the arts who were open to the influences of Italian humanism and Renaissance culture, and who provided a home for the flourishing literature of Dalmatia written in the Croatian language. Like Spalato (Split), where Marko Marulić (1450–1527) worked (he wrote the verse-epic *Judith* there in 1501), she harboured within her walls a number of important poets during the fifteenth, sixteenth and seventeenth centuries. Among these were the romantic lyric writers under the influence of Petrarch, Siško Menčetić (1457–1527) and Djordje Držić (1461–1501), the playwright Marin Držić (1508–1567), and above all Ivan Gundulić (1588–1638), whose baroque epic poem, *Osman*, earned him worldwide fame. It was also in Ragusa that the learned Benedictine abbot Mauro Orbini (*d.* 1614) wrote the first Balkan Slav history, although he limited himself to an uncritical compilation from original sources: it was called *Il regno degli Slavi hoggi corrottamente detti Schiavoni*, and was published in 1601. The work had a lasting effect on the historical consciousness of the Balkan Slavs.

Ragusa's economic and cultural decline began with the terrible earthquake of 1667 from which the city never recovered. Napoleonic troops were to put an end to its autonomous status. In 1814–1815 the city followed the fate of Venice and fell to the Habsburgs.

After the Ottoman conquest of south-eastern Europe, Venice, the one-time proud mistress of the seas, in time found herself confined to a few outposts and the limited area of the city itself and its hinterland, the *terra firma*. The territories remaining to her in the north-east bordered on those areas of the Dalmatian-Croatian kingdom that had survived the collapse of Serbia, Bosnia and Hungary and had managed to resist repeated Ottoman attacks by supporting Habsburg supremacy. The Croatian diet had, for example, voted for the Habsburgs in 1527. This 'remnant of Croatia' included—on the edge of the Austrian crown-lands of

Kranj, Styria and Carinthia–a narrow strip of land reaching up to the rivers Kulpa and Sava via Senj on the coast and Zagreb (Agram) inland, and penetrating to Varaždin. By drawing in fugitives from Turkish-occupied areas, it was replenished with a population tried in battle and willing to fight. These so-called Uskoks (*uskočiti* = to flee) of the Dalmatian coast were notorious and feared equally by friend and foe as they devoted themselves to the profitable business of plunder on the seas from their base in Senj. In the end, after 1557, they became an unbearable menace to the Venetians, and at the beginning of the seventeenth century, having undergone many years of conflict with them, Venice succeeded in making the Habsburgs transfer their settlements from Senj to the interior of the country, to the Karlstadt area and territories by the Kulpa, at the treaty of Madrid.

In this frontier-conscious world there developed a distinctive armed frontier organization, the 'Confine', which had its beginnings in the sixteenth century. A system of fortifications and armed village-type settlements soon developed into a closed settlement area with its administration within the Habsburg union of Austro-Hungary. In the seventeenth and eighteenth centuries this system extended to all the frontier areas bordering on Turkish territory, and reached from the Adriatic coast to Transylvania. The militarized frontier zone played an important part in the process of the integration of the Balkan areas that were being captured from the Turks: by the granting of forms of self-government and special privileges it helped create a class of political leaders among the Slav population. On the other hand, it impaired relations between the central authorities in Vienna and the Slav nationalities by its policy of giving preference to people of German origin for high positions, and by separating the true boundary and its immediate hinterland through the administrative arrangements it engendered.

To leave the 'heroic' lands of the Balkans for a moment, we must here say something of the principalities of Moldavia and Wallachia which lie next to the eastern and southern slopes of the Carpathians. These areas had for long been particularly exposed to the dangers that threatened from the steppes of central Asia, and the formation of independent principalities in the thirteenth and fourteenth centuries had been closely connected with the need for the kingdom of Hungary to secure her frontiers. Under the princes of the Bessarab family, Wallachia was the first to extricate itself from Hungarian tutelage, emerging victorious in battles during the fourteenth century. Moldavia followed its example in the second half of the century. Despite the territory's exposed position between different fronts–that with the Crimean Tatars being to the north, that with the Polish and Hungarian kingdom to the north-west and that with the Ottoman Turks to the south–the native princes maintained their independence by constantly adapting their alliances to meet particular situations and were to a great extent able to survive the general collapse of the Balkan states. Turkish advances across the Danube were successfully repelled by the Wallachian Mircea the Old at the battle in the Olt valley near Rovine against Bayazit I in 1395, as we have seen, and by Stephen the Great of Moldavia (1458–1504) at the memorable battles of Rakova in 1475 and Rebnik in Bukovina in 1481, the dangers which threatened from Hungary being averted by Stephen's victory over Matthias Corvinus at Baja in 1467. In the long run it was impossible for them to avoid making concessions to the superior Ottoman power, especially as the Turkish flag flew over most of Hungary and Transylvania had been reduced to a position of dependence. Already at the beginning of the fifteenth century, after the unsuccessful 'crusade' of Nicopolis, Wallachia had had to submit to paying tribute regularly to the sultan in the treaty of 1411. The most important Moldavian ruler of the Middle Ages, Stephen the Great, advised his successor, Bogdan, to do the same. But with the capitulation of 1513, Bogdan and the princes of Wallachia, in return for recognizing Turkish supremacy, received notable concessions: the right to free election of princes, administrative autonomy, and the right to make their own laws. In this way the Danube principalities managed to enjoy a special position within the Ottoman empire into modern times under their own princes and local aristocracy. The arrangement continued until the court of the sultan began to manipulate the elections of the princes more and more openly. Finally, after the participation of the Danube principalities in Peter the Great's unsuccessful Prut campaign in 1711, it favoured the candidature of foreign Hospodars,[1] which resulted in the supremacy of Greek 'Phanariots' for much of the eighteenth century and well into the nineteenth.

---

[1] Hospodar is the former title of Moldavian and Wallachian princes. (Translator's note.)

7

SOUTH-EASTERN EUROPE UNDER THE TURKISH CRESCENT

The admirable administrative and political skill shown by the Ottoman Turks, the new rulers of the Balkans, both in giving leadership and in guarding the interests of their multi-national empire over several centuries, was never duly or impartially recognized by Balkan historical tradition. The manifest signs of decline in their later years have left a more lasting impression, and the bitterness caused by the wars of independence inevitably gave rise to horror propaganda stories against them that have sullied the reputation of their overlordship ever since.

It was a characteristic of Ottoman rule that it could successfully combine an authoritarian and militaristic form of government with a policy of wide cultural and administrative autonomy for its subject peoples. The political, social, legal and economic exclusiveness of the ruling class in the Balkans, which had always been small in number, was based on its adherence to the religion of Islam. But the fact that Christian renegades, too, were able to attain the highest offices in the land was due to a complete lack of narrow nationalism in the Ottoman political outlook. The capacity of the Turkish empire to recover its strength in times of threatened crisis or disaster can be attributed to its ability to rely on those under its rule. If one excepts the institution of *devshirme* by which Christian boys were conscripted and brought up in the Islamic faith at the court of the sultan, and which was essential for the survival of the janissary corps, forcible attempts at conversion were foreign to the political and legal concepts of Islam. On the other hand, because acceptance of the Islamic faith was directly connected with extensive rights and privileges such as complete exemption from taxes and the right to carry arms, there was a strong incentive for conversion.

The system of land tenure called *spahilik* which was the basis of the Ottoman state was derived from the Byzantine system of *pronoia*, or soldier estates. The transfer of a feudal estate with its subject Christian peasants assured its Muslim owners or *spahi* of their livelihood, and the state of a striking-force of cavalry. According to the size of the leased estate, whether it might be a *khass, ziamet,* or *timar,* the smallest estate, the tenant was obliged to provide a certain body of armed cavalry, or *jebeli*. The Turkish feudal system originally recognized neither inheritance nor privilege of birth; and it was in keeping with the military character of the régime that the feudal estates were integrated with the administrative system, though the hand-over of a feudal estate did not have to be authorized by the administration. The administration itself was frequently supervised by army officers of non-Turkish descent. The *sanjak* ('flag'), the lower administrative division, included all the individual estates in an area. The administrative and military responsibility for a *sanjak* was assigned to a *sanjak-bey* (*beg*), who was in turn responsible to a *beylerbey* (*beglerbeg*), the highest administrative authority. At first this was shared by two pashas, the Beylerbey of Anadolu (that is, of Anatolia, i.e. Asia), and the Beylerbey of Rumeli–i.e. *Rum* or *Rom*, which means territories formerly belonging to the Byzantine empire: the word survives in east Rumelia (southern Bulgaria)– who had his seat in Sofia. In the process of decentralization, various intermediate authorities were merged, several *sanjaks* being joined to *pashaliks* or *vilayets*.

The introduction of the *spahilik* system, which changed the agrarian structure of the Balkan countries, did not, at any rate to begin with, put an impossible burden on the peasants. In many areas the taxes and imposed duties were if anything considerably lower than they had been in earlier centuries. The poll tax went to the state, the produce tax to the master–that on feudal estates going to the *spahi*, that on crown estates to the court of the sultan, and that in the so-called *vakuf* lands to the mosque or the religious foundation concerned. The privileged sections of the non-Muslim population who had special tasks to perform such as the supply of auxiliary troops and the provision of watchmen at bridges and passes and of miners and merchants, could count on some tax relief, and in certain cases on a complete remission of taxes. In the Balkan and Rhodope mountains the so-called *vojnik* villages, the *vojnička sela*, like Koprivštica, Panagjurïste, Kotel, Zeravna, Gradec, Jambol and Sliven became well-known institutions, and they can still be distinguished from other settlements by their layout. They were inhabited by people noted for their self-assurance and economic independence. In the event of war, they were called out as special reserves. At a later period, during the national uprisings, these villages became centres of resistance against foreign domination.

The great majority of the Balkan Christian population, however, were, according to the part of Islamic law relating to aliens, included in the lower class or *raya* (which means 'flock') to indicate that they were under the sultan's care. They were obliged to pay taxes to the Muslim authorities. Their collection and the guaranteeing of revenue from taxes was not the responsibility of Turkish officials but of the church authorities of the different religious communities under the so-called *millet* system. The fact that, because of the religious teachings of Islam, the sultan only had contact with his subjects through the church leaders had significant consequences for the various classes of the population. Ethnic ties were less important in the determination of their social structure than adherence to a religious community.

As the Muslim overlords did not wish to get involved in the internal affairs of the individual *millets*, independent regional authorities were set up over the church organizations to deal with economic and administrative problems. In time, the lines of religious demarcation in south-eastern Europe under Turkish rule became the frontiers for areas of political and national self-determination.

Muslim religious tolerance encouraged a large number of Spanish Jews who had been expelled from Spain to seek refuge in the Ottoman empire, and it also helped to extend the jurisdiction of the Greek patriarch of Constantinople over Orthodox subjects in the Balkans to an unprecedented degree. Some support for national churches did, however, survive within the Orthodox world: in Bulgaria people looked to Ohrid after the decline of the patriarchate of Trnovo from 1393 onwards, and in Serbia to Ipek (Peć). Even so, in 1459 the concept of an independent church had to be given up for a whole century in Serbia. It was to be revived again in 1557 and was then only finally abandoned in 1766. The archbishopric of Ohrid met with the same fate in 1767. In this way, the Greek patriarchate–assisted by the Sublime Porte– achieved supremacy over the Bulgarian and Serbian churches. The ecclesiastical precedence of Constantinople and with it the growth of Greek influence on the hierarchy of the church, on the Christian school system and on the cultural traditions of the Balkan nations adhering to the Orthodox religion must be counted among the most notable results of the Ottoman empire's policy towards the church. Its effects were most marked in Bulgaria and the two Danubian principalities.

For several decades after the fall of Constantinople in 1453, Greek and Byzantine cultural traditions had enjoyed an unexpected revival in Moldavia and Wallachia. It was a matter of 'Byzance après Byzance'. Lively cultural centres sprang up in the many monastic foundations established by the Moldavian princes, the Hospodars, to whose wealth and enterprise splendid manuscripts and unusual frescoes still bear witness. The fifteenth- and sixteenth-century works at Putna, Neamţ, Voroneţ, Moldoviţa, Humor and Suceviţa deserve special mention. The monasteries also offered refuge to many a fugitive from other Balkan countries occupied by the Turks and played a notable role in bringing the Greek cultural heritage into the eastern Slav areas, to Kiev and Moscow. The native boyars in the Danubian principalities completely adopted the Greek way of life and Greek cultural ideals, and lost all connection with their own people. In the eighteenth century, the Turks actually transferred the palaces of the princes in Jassy and Bucharest to distinguished but none the less alien Greeks. It was called the period of the 'Phanariot supremacy' as these Hospodars mostly came from the Phanar, the Greek quarter of Constantinople, and that ensured that the political life of the principalities was subjected to direct Greek influence for a whole century–from

1731 to 1821. It was hardly by accident that the Greek War of Independence in the nineteenth century had its origins in the distant Danubian principalities as well as the Peloponnese. Not till much later when the individual Balkan states had established their political independence did the national churches break away from the jurisdiction and spiritual leadership of the Greek church. Although the Danubian principalities had united in 1861, they did not receive the Greek patriarch's authority for the unilateral proclamation of an independent Romanian Orthodox church until 1865. The Serbian church was to regain its former status of independence in 1879. In Bulgaria, the same issue caused an open break with the oecumenical patriarch, leading to the creation of an independent exarchate in 1870, which was only healed in 1945 when the Greek church gave it an *ex post facto* sanction. It was the close relationship between the people and the lower clergy, whose social status was not very different from that of the lower classes, and the tradition of the nationally based monasteries that enabled a national and religious community to survive the period of Turkish rule. These factors were to give a great impulse to the liberation movements in the Balkan countries of the Orthodox faith.

Five hundred years of Turkish rule in the Christian Balkans had a more easily definable effect in the cultural and social spheres. One clear result was a general tendency for the levelling of social classes. The direct influence of the Orient, however, on language, art, architecture and folklore did not so much create an independent culture in the Balkan interior as isolate it from western medieval and modern influences. The emigration of Albanians to Italy, of Serbs to southern Hungary, and of Croatian, Bosnian and Serbian refugees to territories under Venetian and Habsburg rule did nothing to affect this isolation. The influence of Renaissance humanism only reached as far as Dalmatia, and in general the Reformation penetrated no further than the border of Slovenia and the interior of Croatia, though it had a few small offshoots further to the south, the oecumenical patriarch Kyrillos Lukaris (1621–1638), for instance, showing a receptive attitude towards the teaching of the reformed church. The Slovenes owe the first printed writings in their mother tongue to the unquestioning faith of the church reformers in the language of their people. The first Slovene printing press was founded in 1561 at Urach in Würtemberg by Primož Trubar (1508–1586); further presses were then established, mainly in Tübingen. Of special importance was the translation of the Bible by Juraj Dalmatinac (1547–1589), which appeared in print in Wittenberg in 1584. The church literature of the Habsburg counter-reformation carried out by Jesuits and Franciscans was built up on these foundations, the Franciscans being particularly active and carrying their message far into southern Slav territory. Their sermons and religious writings penetrated right into Bulgaria.

But these influences failed to bring the Balkan countries under Turkish rule into close contact with the spiritual life of western Europe. Between the border areas and the centres of emigration, on the one hand, and the interior of the Balkans, on the other, there developed an antipathy which was to become a serious problem when the nation states developed in the nineteenth century. This antagonism was also reflected in distinctions made between two groups in the interior: first, the privileged population in the autonomous districts and natural defence areas; and second, the largely classless population in the flat part of the country who had been deprived of their aristocratic leaders and had reverted to the life of peasants.

Examples of this kind of reversion and of a return to a patriarchal and more primitive way of life were especially common in the Dinaric region of the western Balkans. In the Serbian and Montenegrin-Albanian areas it was the large family, the *zadruga*, that began to thrive again.

In the towns of the interior, though, the foreign element in ethnic and cultural life grew more pronounced during the period of Turkish rule. Such settlements became the collecting points for a motley mixture of nationalities. At the beginning of the nineteenth century, when the Balkan nations recaptured their lost freedom in a series of sharply contested battles and took their destiny into their own hands, the basis was still lacking for an orderly coexistence of nations because of too little differentiation in the social structure. In the course of a development which was then often too rapid, subsequent generations had to make up for the neglect of previous centuries.

The accomplishments of Turkish rule, by no means always negative as I have said, at first made it easier for the Christian states to accept their fate. There were isolated actions against arbitrary and oppressive measures; ordinary people often venerated and praised heroic fighters in their songs and poetic tales such as the Hajduks in Bulgaria and Serbia, the Uskoks in the north-western Balkans, and the Klephts and Armatoles in Greece and the Macedonian area of Epirus. But as long as the Ottoman military machine functioned and severe reprisals could be expected, it was impossible to rouse the people as a whole to revolt. Even in 1690, Serbian collaborators in the warlike activities of the 'Holy League' that had continued since 1683 were only able to escape Turkish retaliation by a general exodus under the leadership of the patriarch Arsenije III Crnojević of Peć. They moved in mass formation across the Sava and Danube rivers into Hungarian territory, as has been described. It was in this area that the new orthodox Serbian centre around Karlowitz or Karlovci developed, and the Serbian monasteries in Srem in the Fruška Gora were built. Under these conditions, external attempts at intervention by Habsburgs, Venetians, Poles and, later, the Russian tsars could scarcely expect support from within. Their inability to form and co-ordinate concrete war aims, their timid offensive actions, their hasty retreats behind their lines of defence did not inspire sympathy or confidence in the Balkan peoples who were left behind.

The great Austro-Turkish war of 1592–1606 in fact looked like heralding a general change because there was a simultaneous uprising by Michael the Brave (1593–1601) in Wallachia. But the Ottoman empire was able once again to stave off catastrophe and a twenty-year armistice was negotiated at Sitva-Torok in 1606. Then after an incredible renaissance when the Köprülü, the family of a great vizier of Albanian origin – the so-called Arnauts – came back to power, the Turks carried their flag as far as the gates of Vienna, which they subjected to its second siege in 1683. The heroic defence under Rüdiger von Starhemberg and the battle fought at Kahlenberg by a coalition army under Charles of Lorraine and the Polish king Jan III Sobieski coming to his relief initiated the reconquest of the Balkan peninsula by the Habsburgs from Hungary.

In the minds of western Europeans, this heroic period of the Turkish wars and the liberation of Hungary is closely linked with the names of the famous army commanders of the time: prince Eugene of Savoy (1663–1736), the margrave Louis William I of Baden ('the Turkish Louis', 1655–1707), and the Bavarian elector, prince Max Emanuel (Maximilian II Emanuel, 1662–1726), who stormed the city of Belgrade in 1688. The rising Muscovite empire had first of all joined in the great Turkish alliance at the end of the seventeenth century, and had lent a deaf ear to western overtures and requests for assistance from its Orthodox brothers in faith in the Balkans. But the rulers in Moscow were to be forced into a struggle for power with their Turkish neighbours over their acquisitions of territory in the Ukraine and Poland. The Ukrainian acquisitions took place after 1654 and were connected with the great Cossack revolt under Bohdan Khmelnytsky and the treaty of Pereyaslavl; the Polish ones were related to the partitions that took place in the years 1772, 1793 and 1795. Their first concrete results, however, were in no way to the Russian armies' advantage. The campaigns in the Crimea conducted by prince V. V. Golitzin in the years 1687 and 1689 under the tsarina Sofia, and the Prut campaign of Peter the Great in 1711 were unsuccessful.

It was after the end of the seventeenth century that the Balkan problem became more and more clearly an international one, and that it became known in the language of diplomacy as the 'eastern question'. Because of the area's international significance, even after they had gained their independence the Balkan countries only enjoyed a comparative degree of freedom. Their scope was limited by the vital interests of the strong border states of Venice, Austria-Hungary, Poland and Russia and by the near-eastern policies of England as a naval power and France as a continental power. The great powers exploited the increasing readiness of the Balkan peoples during the decline of the Ottoman empire to rise up against harsh exploitation and the greedy self-aggrandisement of individual provincial governors for their own expansionist purposes. For the great powers it was mostly a matter of minor manoeuvres to round off their spheres of influence.

Bourbon France had thus entered into a friendly alliance with the Turks in the sixteenth century by the treaty of 1536: the arch-enemy of the Christian west had become her ally. Her aim was to create a war on two fronts for the Habsburgs, who were her rivals in central Europe. From the end of the eighteenth century onwards strategic and economic considerations such as the route to India and the export trade led British diplomacy, too, to support the Turkish empire. After the great Austrian victories of the seventeenth century and the treaty of Karlowitz in 1699, by which Hungary and Transylvania went to the Habsburgs, the Viennese military authorities were to find that a new rival had emerged for them in the shape of the Russian empire: under Catherine II (1762–1792), the Russians advanced on the Turkish capital of Istanbul. In 1774, the areas between the rivers Dnieper and Bug were annexed by the treaty of Kütchük Kainardji; in 1783, the Crimea was annexed; in 1792, the peace treaty of Jassy bought about the annexation of the area between the Bug and Dniester; in 1812, eastern Moldavia (Bessarabia) was annexed by the treaty of Bucharest. During the campaigns concerned the Russian tsars were able to count on the special sympathy of the Orthodox Christians of the Balkans, their comrades in faith.

It was Napoleon's sally into Egypt in 1799 that finally united the European great powers, leading the arch-enemies, Russia and Turkey, and the rival powers of Austria-Hungary and Great Britain to form a coalition. The nineteenth century was to prove that it was impossible for a single power to solve the eastern question alone. The sharp reactions of rivals and general guarantees on the part of the powers to preserve the Turkish empire, linked with stipulations about the Bosphorus, invariably blocked the way. Such conflicting interests and animosities were to help postpone the collapse of the Turkish empire till the beginning of the twentieth century and preserve an increasingly untenable status quo at the expense of the Balkan Christians.

Russia's further progress as a power in the first half of the nineteenth century–signalled by the treaty of Bucharest (that we have just mentioned) in 1812, by her intervention in the Greek Wars of Independence and her involvement in the treaty of Adrianople in 1829, and by her pact with the sultan of Unkiar Iskelesi in 1833 against the threatened Egyptian secession–was forfeited on the hotly contested ground before the walls of Sebastopol during the Crimean War (1853–1856) to a general European military coalition. The treaty of Paris of 1856 clinched the matter. The exaggerated demands later made by the Russians after their military successes in the Turkish war of 1877–78, instanced by the harsh terms of the treaty of San Stefano and their insistence on the creation of a Greater Bulgarian Empire as the main power in the Balkans, could not be enforced against the combined efforts of European diplomacy to establish a peace that would restore the balance of power–efforts that were crowned at the Congress of Berlin in 1878, with Bismarck as the 'honest broker'. However, there were no adequate foundations on which to build a balance of interests in the Balkans in spite of the fact that the powers concerned, Austria-Hungary and Russia, did make a positive attempt to achieve this during the era of the foreign ministers Goluchovsky (1895–1906) and M. N. Muraviev (1896–1900) (Muraviev being followed by V. N. Lambsdorff, who was foreign minister till 1906). The Goluchovsky-Muraviev agreement of May 1897 aimed at ending rivalry in the Balkans and guaranteeing the status quo. Policies based on a dead pledge and the growing public excitement which some diplomatists did not hesitate to exploit, increased the chances of armed conflict. In May 1906, A. P. Izvolsky took over from Lambsdorff as Russian foreign minister, and in Austria-Hungary count A. Aehrenthal took the place of Goluchovsky in October of that year. The annexation of Bosnia and Herzegovina by Austria-Hungary in 1908 and the ensuing crisis, the 1912 alliance of the Balkan states brought about under Russia's auspices, and the Balkan wars of 1912–13 that followed were all preludes in south-eastern Europe to the first world war, triggered off at

Sarajevo on June 28th, 1914, by the shooting of the heir to the Austro-Hungarian throne– the archduke Franz Ferdinand–and his wife Sophie.

The 'powder keg' of Europe, the Balkan peninsula, only provided the external cause for the war, which was not basically inspired by Balkan problems, though its outcome did radically affect the history of south-eastern Europe. The collapse of three multi-national states, Austria-Hungary, Turkey and Russia, paved the way for far-reaching changes in political relationships there after 1918.

8

NATIONAL REBIRTH

The people of the Balkans did not enter the new heroic age of the Turkish wars unprepared. The songs about their heroes had kept alive the memories of a glorious past; among the Uskoks and Hajduks, a military élite had slowly emerged which had proved itself in face of unfavourable external circumstances. The idea of bringing about a fundamental change in their general conditions by force had already taken root–above all in the autonomous regions tolerated by the Turkish rulers and in the privileged strata of society–because of the awakening self-assurance of the *raya* population. The inhabitants of the *vojnik* villages in Bulgaria, the leaders or *knez* of the self-administered village communities of Serbian peasants under the *knežina* system and the class of tradesmen and merchants with special rights that had formed under the propitious conditions existing in the Ottoman empire guarded their privileges jealously. In the main, it was they who were the champions of armed resistance and revolt–the only effective weapon against the tyranny and corruption that prevailed when the political order collapsed. The Serbian war of independence of 1804 was no chance occurence: it was motivated by local conditions and directed against the despotic rule of a provincial governor.

During the process of social change and re-organization, the closed society of the landed aristocracy was replaced by a new, self-confident class of leaders. This made up for the loss of the indigenous upper class during the first phase of the Turkish conquests and prepared the ground for fresh political activity.

The further away they were from the central government and the nearer to territories ruled by the Venetians and the Habsburgs, the easier it was for such changes to take place among the lawless *raya*.

In Montenegro, formerly Zeta, such a geographical position had had a particularly stimulating effect. Most of the time, the pasha of Scutari had contented himself with nominal rule over the Montenegrin tribes in the highlands. The rebirth of their former patriarchal constitutional system in many localities had gradually forced the leader of the Church, the bishop of Cetinje, to take a more active part in politics to protect his outside interests. Supported by the tribal chiefs, and helped by Venice and the Habsburgs, the bishops in the end took the step of opting out of the Ottoman empire. After the election of Danilo Petrović-Njegoš in 1697, the hereditary office of prince had gone to the family of the bishop, passing from uncle to nephew. The Njegoši dynasty held this exposed position right up to the first world war, preserving and strengthening Montenegrin independence in spite of changing external conditions. Links with the Russian court guaranteed it strong diplomatic support in times of crisis–indeed, from the eighteenth to the early twentieth century, the foreign policy of Montenegro was always orientated towards Russia.

Even greater opportunities for political development were open to the peoples who had settled on the border of the Habsburg union. They had come under Habsburg rule at the end of the seventeenth century with the progressive retreat of the Turks. The movement of the Serbians northwards into Bosnia, Šumadija (Morava-Serbia) and the Sava-Danube area from the fifteenth to the seventeenth century had already caused a profound change in the structure of the agrarian population. Now, the natural hostility between the old settlers and the new arrivals released new social tensions. Austria's general policy in south-eastern Europe, as well as her administrative and social concessions within the military frontier zone, gave the Serbs around the religious centre of Karlovci (Karlowitz) near Srem in southern Hungary and the Croats on the Croatian frontier a chance to drive out pockets of middle class people there who had become the perfect agents for europeanizing the area on the model of the Viennese court and Viennese society. At the same time, the isolation of the Serbian upper class in an unfamiliar environment where a different language from their own was spoken and a different faith prevailed, caused them to look back to their origins and to their historical mission.

The majority of national propagandists among the Serbs, Bulgarians, Romanians and Greeks formed their most important and decisive impressions in such centres of emigration outside the Balkans and they began the process of national rebirth from there. Within the Balkans, it was natural that the new awareness of national origins should have taken root in church circles early on. The daily requirements of spiritual care made it necessary to translate the Christian message into the language of ordinary men and find solutions for their problems and needs. Over centuries of foreign domination, the monasteries had kept close contact with the people in the lands where they were situated, and had fostered the will for national self-determination – as we pointed out in the last chapter. The profession of loyalty to the church by the people was firmly based on social impulses. But in the existing conditions it easily gave place to political demonstrations and activities. From the very beginning, the Turkish aliens' law had allowed for political activity through the *millet* system; under outside influence, it was directed towards the building of nation states.

In the awakening of Romanian nationalism in the Danubian principalities of Moldavia and Wallachia, the role of intermediary was played by Transylvania. That was, for instance, the case with the *Supplex libellus Valachorum transsylvaniensium* of 1791, a petition from Romanians in Transylvania to the emperor Leopold II making nationalistic demands, and with the action taken by the bishops John Micu and Gheorghe Lazăr. A similar role was undertaken by the Serbian element in the kingdom of Hungary for the Serbs still under Turkish domination. Thanks to the imperial privileges they had been granted, especially at the time of the reforms of Maria Theresa and Joseph II, and also to their close cultural ties with Orthodox Russia, the Hungarian Serbs played an important part in the cultural development of Europe in the baroque period and the period of the Enlightenment. From among them came the archimandrate Jovan Rajić (1726–1801), who attempted to give an account of the historical and geographical evolution of the southern Slavs in four volumes published in Vienna in 1794–1795, and the great Serbian intellectual and pioneer in the Serbian language, Dositej Obradović (1742–1811). He–like Rajić–had been a monk on Mount Athos and had only gradually exchanged his ascetic way of life for one concerned with the promotion of worldly cultural ideals. While wandering through Europe he had familiarized himself with the popular ideas of Enlightenment philosophy, and as the first minister of education of an autonomous Serbian principality after 1807 he achieved practical results in the work of creating a nation.

The famous reformer of the Serbian language, Vuk Stefanović Karadžić (1787–1864), who rebelled against Slav church tradition and helped the literature of the popular language to a breakthrough, had his greatest influence abroad when he was an exile in Vienna. His book called *Description of the Serbian Language According to the Speech of the Common Man* was published in 1814/15. His teacher in Vienna, the Slovene slavophil Bartholomeus Kopitar (1780–1844), had urged him to take up the study of the vernacular and had encouraged him to compile a collection of Serbian folk songs, fairy tales and proverbs. Goethe and Grimm expressed much interest in Karadžić's work. The rediscovery of the Serbian people became a European event.

The rebirth of Bulgaria, the *văzraždane*, took place in the face of much severer difficulties. Turkish domination had had a particularly oppressive effect, and the influence exercised by the Greek element in the population on the church, commerce and cultural life generally had concentrated stirrings of national consciousness in the emigré centres north of the Danube at Braila and Bucharest and in the Bulgarian colonies in the big trading centres, Odessa, Smyrna and Constantinople. Father Paisii's *Slaveno-Bulgarian History of the Bulgarian People, Tsars and Saints*, which he wrote in the colloquial idiom in the seclusion of his monastic cell on Athos– first in the Serbian monastery of Chiliandari, and then in the Bulgarian one of Zographou–was completed in 1762. It was a sketch of the nation's history and contained a programme for national reconstruction. Until it was printed in 1844, it had only been circulated in manuscript form. In spite of this, it aroused the

Bulgarian upper class, by now completely 'hellenized', to the rediscovery of the Bulgarian nation and its former greatness. The work of bishop Sofronii of Vraca (1739–1813) was directed to the same end: he wrote an important and tragic autobiography, *The Life and Suffering of the Sinful Sofronii*. Another figure who contributed to the renaissance of national life was the Bulgarian merchant Vasili Aprilov of Odessa, who became the founder of the modern Bulgarian school system. With his business friends Aprilov financed the first Bulgarian school in his home town, Gabrovo. Bulgaria had had close links with Russia and it was this that gave the new intellectual life much of its character.

Croatian nationalism was first associated with the warding off of Hungarian attempts to impose their language and cultural influence. A desire for self-determination was engendered by the creation of a short-lived nation state in the north-western Balkans in the Napoleonic era: the Croatians decided they wanted independence from the Habsburgs and Hungary. Venice's former possessions in Istria and Dalmatia, together with the republic of St. Mark, had fallen into the hands of her ancient rivals, the Habsburgs, under the treaty of Campo Formio in 1797. Then after the treaty of Schönbrunn in 1809, Napoleon's marshal Marmont had united the areas south of the Sava–that is, Slovenia, Trieste, Villach, Kranj, Gorizia and parts of Croatia (the Croatian military frontier zone being retained)–to form a new political entity, the 'Illyrian provinces', with Ljubljana as its capital. As such it only lasted till 1815, but between 1816 and 1849 it continued to exist in modified shape as the 'Illyrian Kingdom' comprising Kranj, Carinthia, Gorizia, Graditsa and Istria within the Habsburg Danube monarchy.

From this union of Slovenes, Croats and Serbs, however temporary it may have been, there grew up a movement among the Croats embodying the ideals of the French Revolution, the ideas of the German romantics and a belief in the pan-Slavism of Kopitar, Palacky and Mickiewicz whose aim was full political unification. Bulgaria was to be among the areas united. The first effective spokesman for this 'Illyrian movement', later to be called the 'southern Slav movement', was Ljudevit Gaj (1809–1872). In his *Short Principles of Croatian-Slav Orthography* written in 1830 he advocated reform of the Croatian alphabet on the lines of the Czech transcription. The plan was to adopt as a basis for the written language a dialect spoken in the largest region of Serbo-Croatia – the so-called *jekavski* version of Štokavski (which is derived from the word *što*, meaning 'what'). This would, to a great extent, bring the language into line with the Serbian language reforms of Vuk Karadžić. It would also help establish a closer union between the two nations. But the Croatian ideal of an 'Illyrian Kingdom' could not stand up against the Serbian dream of a 'Greater Serbia' and against Habsburg centralization. The bishop of Djakovo, J. J. Strossmayer, who by founding the 'Yugoslav Academy' at Zagreb in 1867 had showed that he favoured the campaign for the unification of the southern Slavs, found that his hopes of creating a federal union in the Habsburg empire and granting concessions to all nationalities were to become more and more illusory. Harsh experience taught the Croats that such concessions could never be obtained without first reaching a settlement with the Hungarians. That they were finally to achieve in 1868.

The case of the Croats made it very clear just how much scope there was for national movements among the Balkan peoples under the Habsburg monarchy. The centralized Austrian empire had for centuries exploited the loyalty to the crown of the frontier population in the Croatian military border zone, balancing it against the class interests of the civilian Hungarian-Croat nobility in the kingdom of Croatia-Slavonia. When the Hungarian-Croat aristocracy, in negotiation with foreign powers (Turkey included), had been hoping to gain recognition for the special constitutional position of Hungary and its neighbouring countries, the emperor Leopold I (1658–1705) had stepped in with a firm hand. In 1671 he had had the magnates Peter Zrinski, or Zrinji, and Krsto Frankopan, or Frangipani, executed in Wiener Neustadt. However, the aims and ideas of the conspirators, who also included the count palatine, Franz-Wesselényi, and the magnates Nádasdy, Tököly and Rákóczy, were not easily suppressed. They were kept alive through the uprising under Franz II Rákóczy and count

Emmerick Tököly leading to the 'Kuruzzi' wars of 1704–1711. In their resistance to the centralizing tendencies of the Viennese court, the Croatian and Hungarian aristocracy had joined together in an alliance of convenience; but with the increase of Hungarian influence after the beginning of the eighteenth century, when the official language was changed from Latin to Hungarian and education, commerce, and the administration came progressively under Hungarian control, it underwent a severe testing.

In the year of revolution, 1848, all the non-Hungarian nationalities under the Habsburg monarchy refused to follow the popular leader, Louis Kossuth, in his aggressive nationalism. And the next year, the Viennese government managed to defeat Kossuth's national army, 'Honvéd', which capitulated at Világos, through the intervention of the Russian tsar, Nicholas I, and with the assistance of Serbian, Romanian and Slovak volunteers and Croatian troops under the Ban, general Joseph Jelačić. Even so, two decades later Hungary was to achieve self-government within the framework of the Danube monarchy at the famous 'settlement' of 1867.

In the period following, Hungarian nationalism became intolerant of policies of national independence in spite of the agreement made with the Croats in 1868: all efforts to create a federal state out of the nations concerned invariably foundered in the chauvinistic drive of the Hungarians for the status of a great power. The Serbian foreign minister Ilija Garašanin's dreams of a rebirth of Stefan Dušan's empire–revealed in the famous secret document of 1844, the 'Načertanje'–had found many enthusiastic supporters among the youth movement of the 1860s, 'Omladina'. On the other hand, Croatian ideas of Illyrian unity had lost much of their popularity with the rise of the nationalist independence party of Ante Starčević (d. 1896).

Despite the eventual liquidation of the multi-national Ottoman and Austro-Hungarian states in south-eastern Europe, no permanent equivalent structure was created. There was to be no great power with a truly national basis. Svetozar Marković (1846–1875), who had supported the ideas of the Omladina movement for a greater Serbia and had committed himself to the materialistic and socialist thought of his times, predicted that the revolutionary movements among the subject Balkan peoples would be successful, and that a new phase of political rebirth lay ahead. But the uncoordinated aims of the various national revolutions prevented them from achieving the vital solidarity they needed.

9

ON THE ROAD TO THE
NATION STATE

The slow dawning of national consciousness, tinged with romanticism, that took place among the Balkan peoples found nothing to direct it in the political life of the region. The ideas of the French Revolution and the German Romantics had inspired the will to establish an independent nation state, as we saw, but it was in an area where separate states had maintained their separate traditions for five hundred years. The romantic idea of reviving the medieval 'empire' and achieving great national objectives was therefore incapable of realization because of the antagonism that existed between the different nationalities and minorities. A serious impediment to the creation of a new order of Balkan nations was the fact that, in times of conflict, national groups put their individual irredentist aims before those of the population as a whole.

The internal weakness of the states was proved by their only being able to free themselves from Ottoman domination in the nineteenth century through more or less openly accepting the protection of one of the neighbouring great powers–either Austria-Hungary or Russia. Owing to the similarity between their religions, many of them looked for support to Orthodox Russia, who since the end of the eighteenth century had skilfully allowed herself to be pushed into the role of protector of Orthodox Christianity under Turkish rule. Since Peter the Great, Russian agents had sought closer contact with the *raya* population, bypassing Turkish officialdom. In the 1840s, Odessa played an important part in creating a new, self-confident intelligentsia in Bulgaria. The close relationship between the Serbian Orthodox patriarch of Karlovci in southern Hungary and the Russian Orthodox church was plain not only from the literature and cultural life of the Serbs there; many of them also responded to the appeals of tsarist officials and moved as settlers into the newly acquired Russian territory in the northern Black Sea area – 'New Serbia'. However, relations between the Balkan countries and Russia were on the whole no less disappointing than those with the Habsburgs.

The first revolutionary movement among the Christian *raya* at Šumadija in 1804, which heralded the period of Balkan national uprisings, became part of the conflict between the great powers. The trouble had flared up because of the abuses and incompetence of the local Turkish administration in the *pashalik* of Belgrade. In order to defend himself against the arbitrary rule of the janissaries (the Dahis), who had found support from their neighbour the governor of the province of Vidin, Pasvan Oglu, the pasha of Belgrade had as a last resort called the Serbian peasants to arms under the command of their *knez*. After a terrible massacre of the peasant leaders by the janissaries, the extent of which was suppressed, Djordje Petrović, 'Black George' or Karadjordje, put himself at the head of a popular rising. He was from the new middle class of Šumadija Serbs, and as a former Hajduk who had been in the service of the Austrian army he had already fought against the Turks and proved himself a leader.

His movement lacked clearly defined political aims. The peasants' emotions were not directed against the sultan in far-away Istanbul but against the manifest abuses of the janissaries' rule in the *pashalik* of Belgrade. However, the lack of sympathy shown at the sultan's court for the demands of autonomy made by the rebels – who soon gained control of the most important places such as Šabac, Požarevac (or Passarovitz), Smederevo and Belgrade – turned the dispute into a revolution. Because of the international situation at the beginning of the nineteenth century outside help was slow in coming. Only the Serbs in southern Hungary and some Austrian officers of Serbian descent put themselves unhesitatingly at the disposal of the Serbian rebels. The Habsburgs were busy with their quarrels with Napoleon in France as it was the early phase of the war of the third coalition; and the Russian tsar Alexander I became entangled in a new war with the Turkish

Map 8. The Ottoman and Austro-Hungarian empires, 1815

1	Kingdom of Bohemia and Moravia	10	Banat
2	Kingdom of Galicia	11	Transylvania
3	Moldavia	12	Wallachia
4	Bessarabia	13	Kingdom of Sardinia
5	Kingdom of Bavaria	14	Lombardy
6	Switzerland	15	Venetia
7	Tyrol	16	Duchy of Parma
8	Kingdom of Illyria	17	Duchy of Modena
9	Slavonia	18	Corsica
		19	Grand Duchy of Tuscany
20	States of the Church	28	Albania
21	Kingdom of Dalmatia	29	Rumelia
22	Bosnia	30	Thessaly
23	Herzegovina	31	Livadia
24	Principality of Serbia	32	Morea
25	Bulgaria	33	Crete
26	Kingdom of the Two Sicilies		
27	Principality of Montenegro		

empire in 1806, and after the agreements made with Napoleon at Tilsit on July 7th, 1807, and at Erfurt on October 12th, 1808, he refrained from taking sides openly in the internal squabbles of the Balkans.

The already divided Serbian ruling class was further split by the growing controversy as to whether it should pursue a pro-Austrian or a pro-Russian policy. At the treaty of Bucharest of 16th/28th May, 1812, the Russians negotiating with the sultan were content to accept a formal guarantee for the autonomous state of Serbia, and a general amnesty for all rebels. Turkish troops had then marched in on the area of rebellion. At this, Karadjordje had gone over into Austrian territory in 1813, leaving the leadership of his people to the cautious tactician Miloš Obrenović, who was prepared to compromise and did not shy from temporary collaboration with the Turks. The ultimate success of Obrenović the artful diplomat, and the failure of the national hero Karadjordje throw a revealing light on the Balkan political situation during the movements for independence. A clever combination of evolutionary and revolutionary measures turned out to be more effective than the unleashing of spontaneous, non-political revolutionary enthusiasm.

The uncompromising feud between the families of the Karadjordević and Obrenović, already apparent at this early stage of Serbia's revolution, was to overshadow the development of the new principality and its monarchy. Out of nine rulers in Serbia and Yugoslavia during the nineteenth and twentieth centuries, four died violent deaths and four were driven from the throne and forced to abdicate.

Suspicion rested on Karadjordje for having had a hand in the death in 1810 of Milan Obrenović, Miloš' half-brother, who had surrounded himself with a pro-Russian faction. To avenge him, Miloš had Karadjordje murdered in 1817. Nevertheless, the Karadjordjevićs returned to the throne temporarily in the middle of the century in 1842–1859, and from 1903 onwards they occupied it permanently.

With Turkish support, Miloš Obrenović had himself confirmed as *knez* of the Serbs. Then in a second evolutionary phase after

1815, he led the Serbs in a slow ascent to full independence. Favourable circumstances had made his attempt to steer a middle course between the powers considerably easier. The Greek War of Independence that had begun in 1821 was finally brought to a successful conclusion on the crest of a wave of pro-Greek sympathy in the western world. The war was effective in extorting from the sultan many concessions for his other Christian subjects, too. At the Russo-Turkish treaty of Adrianople in September 1829, the tsar insisted on the strict observance of Serbian autonomy, which had been promised at Bucharest in 1812. His position as protector of the Danubian principalities was again expressly confirmed as well. This meant the end of the dominance in Moldavia and Wallachia of the Greek Phanariots, who were dependent on the Turks, and the election of native princes for life instead. In August 1830, the sultan carried out his Serbian obligations: Miloš Obrenović was recognized as prince of an autonomous Serbia; the sultan's sovereign rights were limited to the occupation of certain frontier fortresses and the receipt of payments of tribute.

At the beginning of the nineteenth century, then, large areas of the Balkan peninsula were withdrawn from direct Turkish control: first Greece, next the Romanian principalities by the Danube and then the Serbian principality–which merely comprised the areas around Belgrade and the northern valley of the Morava to begin with. In the case of Montenegro, too, a state of dependency had long been a thing of the past, since the moment when the theocratic regime of the bishops of Cetinje had asserted itself in 1697 under bishop Vladika Danilo Petrović. However, neither participation in the Turkish wars at the end of the eighteenth century nor military successes alongside the Russians at the beginning of the nineteenth (e.g. the capture of Kotor in 1812) had brought her lasting guarantees that were valid under international law. Peter I Petrović (1782–1830) deserves credit for the efforts he made to bring peace to a land torn by racial feuds. His nephew Peter II Petrović (1830–1851) was to do much to promote cultural life, and with his poem, *The Mountain Wreath* (Gorski Vijenac, 1847), he added a masterpiece to Serbian literature. Danilo I Petrović (1851–1860), Peter II's successor, having resigned the holy office of bishop, declared his country a hereditary principality with Austrian and Russian consent and continued the work of building up its independent position.

Despite substantial reforms in favour of the Christian *raya*, the Turks failed to prevent the collapse of their empire. The efforts of Selim III (1789–1807) were wrecked by reactionary powers within. By meeting resistance with a bloody campaign of terror, highlighted by the extermination of the janissaries in 1826, his successor, Mohammed II (1808–1839), showed the way to overcome internal anarchy. The decree of reform promulgated in 1839 by the next sultan, Abdul Medshid (1839–1861), the *Hatti-i-sherif* of Gülhané, introduced the true period of reform, the *Tanzimat*. But time was not on the side of the far-sighted reformers, among whom Reshed Mustafa Pasha showed exceptional statesmanlike qualities. Even the granting of full equal status by the *Hatti-i-humajun* of 1856 could not halt the secessionist movement in the Christian Balkans. By now the whole empire was beginning to disintegrate. Twice, in 1831–1833 and 1839–1841, Mohammed Ali had set out from his Egyptian headquarters to strike a death blow at its centre. It had only been the energetic intervention of the great powers that had enabled the main body of the empire to survive this difficult period and hold off the Russians during the Crimean war of 1853–56. At the treaty of Paris in 1856, the territorial integrity of the Turkish empire was guaranteed by the European powers. But still, the Romanian nationalities in Moldavia and Wallachia suffered no ill consequences when in 1859 they disregarded important provisions of the treaty and elected general Alexander Cuza, who later united the two principalities in 1861 and so founded a Romanian national state. To start off with, this state remained formally under Turkish rule. In 1866, prince Charles von Hohenzollern-Sigmaringen took over the leadership from Cuza, and in 1881 he was crowned king.

It was on the battlefields of Europe at the end of the 1860s and the beginning of the 1870s that the international balance of power, established by the Paris treaty in order to guarantee the territories and straits under Turkish control, broke down. The Austrian empire had been considerably weakened by its defeats in Italy at

Magenta and Solferino in 1859 and by the battle of Königsgratz against the Prussians in 1866. After the Franco-Prussian war of 1870–1871, Russia–with Bismarck's approval–had denounced the burdensome provisions of the treaty relating to the Bosphorus in October 1873. Bismarck's hopes that the close alliance of the conservative eastern powers achieved by the alliance of the 'three emperors' on October 22nd, 1873, would put the European power system on a more lasting footing through territorial saturation and cordial understanding between monarchs, were thwarted because of the unresolved eastern question.

Growing concern at the self-seeking policies of the European powers in the Balkans brought about a community of interests among the independent and semi-independent nations of south-eastern Europe as early as the beginning of the 1860s. On the initiative of the Greeks, talks had begun between the Serbian and Greek governments in 1860–1861. Although there was extensive agreement on the question of the creation of a defensive and offensive alliance, and on non-intervention in internal Balkan affairs on the part of the great powers, the harmony achieved was destroyed by exaggerated territorial demands. Serbia demanded large areas of Bulgaria. Greece laid claim to Macedonia and Thrace. However, Michael Obrenović (1860–1868), probably the most important figure in modern Serbian history, did not allow himself to be deflected by such demands and carried through a programme for united action in a series of bilateral agreements. In putting to the vote decisions concerning the conflicting interests of Greece, Montenegro, Romania, Serbia and the Bulgarian Revolutionary Committee, he showed remarkable negotiating skill. His murder in 1868 deprived the first Balkan alliance of its most important leader, although it actually occurred at a point when there was no longer a propitious climate for such an alliance since it was the time of the Austro-Prussian war and of the rebellion in Crete of 1866.

In 1875, barely a decade later, an uprising in Bosnia and Herzegovina led to a major Balkan crisis which began a new, decisive phase in the movement for national independence. It was the beginning of an ideological change in the revolutionary programme, which had received much impetus from the revolution of 1848 and from European liberalism and constitutionalism. Especially among the young Balkan intellectuals, these had aroused feelings of political and social solidarity, with strong overtones of romanticism and panslavism, and that had resulted in the founding of the Serbian Omladina movement at Novi Sad in 1866. In addition, the positivist and, in social affairs, utopian ideas of the Paris Commune and the radical Russian critique of society to be found in the works of Chernichevsky and Dobroljubov had penetrated to Serbia through Svetozar Marković, and to Bulgaria through Christo Botev.

The particular social conditions in Bosnia and Herzegovina and deliberate agitation in the Serbian and Montenegrin armies, coupled with the Habsburg desire to annex further territories, produced a revolutionary situation which was bound to end in open conflict.

Over the centuries, Bosnia had held a special position among the Turkish provinces of the Balkan peninsula like Albania. The conversion of her local nobility to the Muslim faith had preserved an upper class which, though it had developed naturally, had nevertheless become more and more estranged from the common people. It was this aristocracy that at a time of growing Balkan nationalism had become the most zealous defender of an all-embracing Turkish state. The economic reprisals that were a direct consequence of Bosnia's internal crisis, and the existing religious antagonism, had led to a general mobilization of the people under revolutionary slogans and provided many opportunities for agitation. When the revolt broke out in Herzegovina in July 1875 and spread quickly, Montenegro offered military assistance. Prince Nicolas I of Montenegro (1860–1918) had been forced into open intervention under pressure from an excited populace. In Serbia, Milan Obrenović (1868–1889, and king from 1882 onwards) was in a similar position, for there Jovan Ristić had openly steered a collision course after the success of the liberals at the elections. On June 30th, 1876, Serbia declared war on Turkey. On July 2nd, Montenegro followed suit. The war was soon to take an unfavourable turn for the Balkan countries, however, and finally it involved Russia who declared war on April 27th, 1877.

All this had been preceded by a period of hectic diplomatic activity against a background of rapprochement between the courts of Vienna and St. Petersburg and of a sharpening of the tension between Russia and England. The agreement reached between the Austro-Hungarian and Russian foreign ministers, Andrássy and Gorchakov, at Reichstadt on July 8th, 1876, had provided for the restoration of the status quo in the event of a Serbian defeat, and for checks on the emergence of a super-power in the Balkans in the event of a Turkish defeat. It had also allowed some territorial adjustments in favour of the Habsburgs in Bosnia and Herzegovina, and of Russia in Bessarabia (or eastern Moldavia) and Asia Minor. The readiness on the part of the great powers to intervene was reinforced by incidents attracting much attention during the unsuccessful rising in Bulgaria.

As far as the Balkan liberation movement was concerned, the Bulgarians had much lost ground to make up. Bulgaria's special internal and external conditions had delayed her transition from national consciousness to development of a common political will for generations. The winning of emancipation from the spiritual supremacy of the Greek patriarch had for decades absorbed most of the nation's energies. The support of pan-Slav circles in Russia, the powerful emigré population in Bucharest and Braila, and the Bulgarian community in Constantinople made it impossible to ignore demands for separation of the Bulgarian Orthodox church from the tutelage of the Greek patriarchate. In the 1860s the struggle between the churches had become more violent, so that even the sultan's court could no longer afford to ignore the desire for a permanent settlement of their disputes. The growth of the concept of a 'Greater Bulgaria' was apparent behind these demands for the demarcation of a Bulgarian diocese. In the end, a commission had been set up composed of Turkish officials and the Russian representative Ignatiev. From March 11th, 1870, onwards the sultan's *firman* granted the Christian population the choice between the Greek church and the newly created Bulgarian church. It gave considerable moral encouragement to Bulgarian hopes. But in spite of the decision, the Greek patriarch did not acknowledge the existence of the Bulgarian national church and refused official church recognition of the Bulgarian exarchate. It was not till 1945 that its ban was lifted.

The political emancipation of the Bulgarian people from Turkey did not at first keep pace with its spiritual emancipation. The efforts of the 'reformers'–mostly recruited from the politically active middle class of teachers, craftsmen and merchants–to achieve a settlement were in the long run more successful than the isolated attempts at rebellion that had been made between 1830 and 1850. The majority of the country people still refused to accept the radical ideas of revolutionary agitators such as Georgi Rakovski, Ljuben Karavelov, Vasil Levski, Christo Botev and Stefan Stambulov. Nevertheless, their widespread underground activities fostered the necessary conditions and prepared the necessary organization for the coming revolution, which was promoted from Romanian soil across the Danube by groups of exiles.

Karavelov and Levski had set up a revolutionary committee in Bucharest in 1871, but they had been betrayed to the authorities and prevented from carrying out their plans. In 1875, the news of the revolt in Bosnia and Herzegovina had encouraged Botev and Stambulov in their preparations for a new attempt at rebellion. This broke out on May 2nd in the *vojnik* villages of Panagjurište and Koprivštica in the Balkan mountains. However, a sudden decision to bring the date for the rebellion forward, the inadequate preparations and organization for it, and a number of important tactical mistakes allowed the Turkish troops who had been alerted to regain control of the situation swiftly. If neither side was innocent of atrocities, the bloody acts of suppression and harsh measures of retaliation carried out by the Turks left a far deeper impression on contemporary opinion. The 'Bulgarian outrage' gave the neighbouring states, who were ready to intervene, a welcome justification in the eyes of the public. What was more significant, they tied the hands of Disraeli's government. Powerless to do anything, it had to watch Russia enter the war and then march to victory in the Balkans.

In return for Russia's assurances in respect of their subsequent occupation of Bosnia and Herzegovina, the Austrians promised to adopt a position of benevolent neutrality at the Convention of Budapest on January 15th, 1877. On June 19th, 1877, Russian troops forced their way across the Šipka pass into the south Bulgarian plain; the hotly contested city of Plevna fell on December 10th; and in January, 1878, the armies stood before Istanbul. The sultan was forced to begin negotiations for a cease-fire, in the course of which the Russian plenipotentiaries at San Stefano near Istanbul dictated tough peace conditions on March 3rd, 1878: Serbia, Montenegro and Romania were to be allowed complete independence and some enlargement of their territories, while the remaining Turkish possessions in the Balkan peninsula, including Macedonia, were to be incorporated into an autonomous Bulgarian principality.

The establishment under Russian patronage of a 'Greater Bulgarian Empire' as the leading power in the Balkans not only ran counter to the agreement with the Habsburgs. It was also bound to arouse bitter opposition among the other Balkan countries. British and Austrian diplomacy therefore found support for their demand that the eastern question should be resolved by international arbitration after the end of the Russo-Turkish war. From June 13th to July 13th, 1878, the representatives of the signatories to the Paris peace treaty of 1856 assembled in Berlin under the chairmanship of Bismarck. New peace arrangements for south-eastern Europe were concluded. But the countries most concerned were excluded from the deliberations.

Disraeli had good reason to feel that he had in reality won a diplomatic victory over Russian imperialism in the Near East since it proved impossible to find a permanent solution to the Balkan problem during the heated debates in Berlin. No compromise between the strongly divergent opinions could be achieved in the Congress resolutions. On the contrary, the resolutions contributed to further complications. The displeasure in St. Petersburg at Bismarck's lack of understanding produced a marked coolness in Russo-German relations, the immediate result being Germany's closer support for Austro-Hungarian policy in the alliance of 1879. By occupying Bosnia, Herzegovina and the *sanjak* of Novipazar, the Austro-Hungarian empire assured for itself key positions in the

Map 9. The Balkans after the Congress of Berlin in 1878

1 Brindisi
2 Bari
3 Linz
4 Vienna
5 Pressburg
  (Bratislava)
6 Graz
7 Budapest
8 Czernowitz
  (Chernovtsy)
9 Kishinev
10 Jassy (Iaşi)
11 Galaţi
12 Kronstadt
  (Braşov)
13 Hermannstadt
  (Sibiu)
14 Orşova
15 Temesvár
  (Timişoara)

16 Arad
17 Klausenburg
  (Cluj)
18 Szeged
19 Fünfkirchen
  (Pécs)
20 Essego (Osijek)
21 Zagreb (Agram)
22 Laibach
  (Ljubljana)
23 Fiume (Rijeka)
24 Zara (Zadar)
25 Spalato (Split)
26 Sarajevo
27 Belgrade
28 Niš
29 Vidin
30 Bucharest
31 Constanza
32 Silistria
33 Varna
34 Sofia

35 Philippopolis
  (Plovdiv)
36 Burgas
37 Ragusa
38 Cattaro
39 Cetinje
40 Dulcigno
41 Scutari
42 Peć
43 Priština
44 Prizren
45 Skopje

46 Strumica
47 Durazzo
48 Tirana
49 Valona
50 Yannina
51 Arta

52 Patras
53 Athens
54 Larissa
55 Salonika
56 Adrianople
  (Edirne)
57 Istanbul
58 Bursa
59 Smyrna (Izmir)

new political order in south-eastern Europe. A formal state of independence and some modest territorial gains for the principalities of Serbia, Montenegro and Romania did not compensate for the disappointment felt in these countries at the lack of consideration given to their nationalist hopes.

The national pride of the Bulgarians was particularly hurt. They saw themselves confined to the territories between the Balkan mountains and the Danube in an autonomous principality under Turkish suzerainty; while eastern Rumelia (which became a Turkish province with administrative autonomy) and Thrace were again lost to the Turks. The thwarted nationalism of the Balkan peoples sought an outlet in the terrorism of the irredentist movement. In the following decades, both the dream of a great empire based on nationality and revolutionary solidarity were increasingly sacrificed in a bitter struggle for power. The solution for their problems was to be found in the making of adjustments in response to changes in the European power balance. The demarcation of Austro-Hungarian and Russian spheres of influence in the south-east by the renewal of the treaty between the 'three emperors' on June 18th, 1881, was closely reflected during the next few years in the foreign policies of Serbia and Bulgaria. Disappointed by Russian policy towards Bulgaria, Serbia turned to an alliance with Habsburg Austria and for the time being gave up her claims to Bosnia and Herzegovina. After the conclusion of the trade treaty of April 21st, 1881, she was to become economically dependent for ten years on her northern neighbour, the Danube monarchy, which was to account for eighty-seven per cent of her exports and sixty-seven per cent of her imports. A secret treaty of the same year gave Austria-Hungary special rights with regard to Serbian foreign policy. By similar agreements, Austro-Hungarian policy managed to secure control over the foreign policies of Romania in 1883 and Greece in 1885.

To meet this situation, the Bulgarians embarked on a strategy of close collaboration with Russian tsarism. It was felt that strong Russian support would ensure the re-establishment of the frontiers of San Stefano which had been lost at the Congress of Berlin. In return, Russian diplomacy hoped that the new Bulgarian prince,

Alexander von Battenberg, who was related to the Russian royal family, and the liberal constitution of Trnovo of 1879 would between them provide the personal and constitutional climate needed for an active Balkan policy in the near future.

The complete futility of Russia's policy became apparent the first time it was put to the test. When a revolutionary uprising in eastern Rumelia proclaimed a union with the autonomous Bulgarian principality, prince Alexander gave in to national pressure and, in conscious defiance of the decisions of the Congress of Berlin, placed himself at the head of the Bulgarian unification movement. He did not allow himself to be diverted from his purpose by either warnings from or direct intervention by the Russian government. Tsar Alexander III recalled all Russian officers and instructors from Bulgaria, depriving the Bulgarian army of almost its complete military leadership at a single blow. But its spectacular victory at Slivnica on November 17th–19th, 1885, against the Serbian invading forces who were meant to give support to king Milan's demands for compensation, ensured international backing not only for the leadership of the national army but also for Bulgarian territorial expansion. Russia found herself faced with a union of eastern Rumelia and Bulgaria—at first to be limited to a period of five years. Great Britain had from the beginning raised no objections, in contrast to her position at the Congress of Berlin. Even the sensational circumstances in which the Russian tsar staged a violent abduction in August 1886 and forced Alexander von Battenberg to renounce the throne, failed to win back Russia's lost position in Bulgaria.

As the leading statesman in the next decade, Stefan Stambulov, the Bulgarian prime minister from 1887 to 1894, exploited the anti-Russian sentiments of the Bulgarians to the benefit of his national party and, against the will of the tsar, worked for the recognition of the newly elected ruler, Ferdinand of the house of Saxe-Coburg-Gotha-Koháry (1887–1918). However, Ferdinand quarrelled with his overbearing and unscrupulous minister in 1894 —Stambulov was murdered in the street a year after his dismissal— and sought a reconciliation with Russia. This move helped him win international recognition for his position in 1896. But neither over his general foreign policy nor over the Macedonian question, which involved the other Balkan countries, did he find the support he had hoped for.

By contrast, the repressive economic measures adopted after 1906 followed by the crisis over the annexation of Bosnia in 1908 and the diplomatic developments during the Balkan wars of 1912–1913 set the final seal on the estrangement of Austria-Hungary and its Serbian ally. As the inevitable consequence of a changing world, there began a complete transformation of the Balkan system of alliances. The end result was that Bulgaria was drawn into the first world war on the side of Austria-Hungary against Serbia, who was the ally of Russia.

The history of the Balkans from 1878 until well into the twentieth century was to be largely governed by unresolved frontier problems.

10

BALKAN IRREDENTISM:
THE BALKAN CRISIS

After 1878, the Ottoman empire was clearly falling apart, and the foreign policies of the new Balkan countries were irretrievably drawn into the devil's net of irredentism. The dream of a system of nation states was to turn into a feverish race to divide up the remaining Turkish territories in Europe, and petty wrangling over frontier realignments and the re-allocation of land.

The mixture of nationalities in a number of recently disputed areas had made it impracticable to draw exact and satisfactory frontiers between them. Strategic and economic considerations such as free access to the sea had rendered excited nationalists in all camps unwilling to accept the existing conditions, which were haphazard and arbitrary. The Transylvanian question divided Hungary and Romania. There were Bulgarian and Romanian interests in Bessarabia, and Bulgarian and Greek ones in Thrace. In the twentieth century, the Yugoslav government was to have to defend its frontiers against Hungary in the Vojvodina (southern Hungary) and against Albania in Kosovo-Metohija; and it was to lay claim to Trieste and Istria from Italy. Also, the Habsburgs had for many decades refused to allow the incorporation of Bosnia, Herzegovina and the *sanjak* of Novipazar into Serbia; while the kingdom of Greece had attempted with parallel tenacity to extend its northern frontier towards southern Albania, that is, to northern Epirus.

Macedonia was the classic example of the warring of national groups in the Balkans at the end of the nineteenth century. Bulgaria, Serbia and Greece all laid equal claim to the country. Because of its singular strategic and economic importance, neighbouring states hoping to expand looked in its direction. Macedonia not only dominated an important line of communications, the route along the Vardar, but it also had contact through the port of Salonica with commercial centres in the Aegean and the Mediterranean. In the population of the Turkish *vilayets* of Salonica, Monastir and Kosovo, the Slav element was unquestionably predominant, although there were Greek, Albanian, Turkish, Kutzo-Wallachian and Jewish minorities. The dialect, however, of the Slav majority was not sufficient justification for their joining forces with their Serbian or Bulgarian neighbours. At the turn of the century the prerequisites were lacking for any proper 'Macedonian' solution to the country's problems, such as a written language or a real sense of community; they were not in evidence until Tito came to power in Yugoslavia.

Increasing emigration to Bulgaria and the extension of the Bulgarian exarch's jurisdiction to Macedonia ensured a head start for Bulgarian nationalism and Stambulov's Macedonian policy over the endeavours of the Greeks and the Serbs. The 'External Organizing Committee', made up of Bulgarian emigrés and founded in Sofia in 1895, urged that the Macedonian question should be resolved by the military in the interests of Bulgarian nationalism. On the other hand, the 'Internal Macedonian Revolutionary Organization' (the I.M.R.O.), after preliminary hesitation, supported a 'Macedonian' federal solution, by which an undivided, autonomous Macedonia would be an equal member in a Balkan federation, as a way out of the dilemma produced by the gang warfare between the different nationalists in the 1890s – the 'Society of Saint Sava' having been founded in Serbia in 1886, and the 'National Society', the Ethnikē Hetaireia, in Athens in 1894. At the height of the terrorism, after the I.M.R.O. rising on Eliasday (August 2nd), 1903, Austria-Hungary and Russia intervened to preserve the status quo, backing a Turkish policy of reform for Macedonia. Their policy was confirmed by the treaty of Mürzsteg of October 1903 (Mürzsteg being an imperial shooting lodge near Neuberg in Styria). It was not to prove any more lasting than the Serbo-Bulgarian rapprochement after the murder of the king of Serbia.

On June 10th, 1903, the last of the Serbian Obrenović, the unsuccessful Alexander, had fallen a victim to an officers' conspiracy. Because of her entanglements in the Far East leading to the

Russo-Japanese war of 1904–1905, Russia could not give any effective support to the new ruler, Peter Karadjordjević (1903–1921), who attempted to counterbalance Austria-Hungary's negative attitude by concluding a secret military alliance with Bulgaria on April 12th, 1904, and a trade agreement with her on June 22nd, 1905. Serbia was to weather the unexpected trade embargo of the Viennese government that followed, the so-called 'Pig War' of June 1906 to 1909, by reorganizing its trade relations and creating its own meat-processing industry. In such a way, the uncompromising attitudes of Viennese diplomacy contributed to changes in the Balkan system of alliances, which began to crumble soon after the events of the crisis year of 1908.

In July 1908, a conspiracy of Turkish officers at Salonica in Macedonia had compelled the autocratic sultan Abdul Hamid to restore constitutional government to Turkey. After then successfully resisting a conservative counter-revolution, the officers had taken over the government. On April 27th, 1909, the sultan abdicated, his successor, Mehmed V (1909–1918), being left with but limited powers. The national reform programme of the 'Young Turks' Revolution' which was aimed at preserving the territory of the Ottoman empire against the newly awakened nationalism of Armenia, Crete, the Balkan peninsula and the Arab countries, was, however, largely a failure. For the chaos at the centre stimulated the desire to break away, as was shown by the Albanian uprising of 1910. It also led the great powers to the realization that the 'eastern question' had to be cleared up once and for all.

It was in anticipation of territorial changes in south-eastern Europe that the Austrian foreign minister, count A. Aehrenthal, created a totally new situation by officially annexing Bosnia and Herzegovina on October 5th, 1908. The day before, Ferdinand of Bulgaria had declared his country independent, and had assumed the title of tsar.

The crisis that arose over the annexation was in fact settled by diplomatic means since neither of the two neighbouring countries most affected—Serbia and Turkey—nor Russia as a power in the background, were ready to take up arms. But its indirect repercussions were serious. Animosity among the Serbs towards the

Habsburg Danube monarchy was generated; Russian-Austrian antagonism over south-eastern Europe which had lain buried for a decade was revived, though it had already shown signs of re-emerging at the time of the Austrian Sanjak-railway project; a Balkan alliance was formed; the Balkan wars of 1912–13, the assassination at Sarajevo and the outbreak of the first world war followed. The European balance of power had been so utterly upset that it could not be restored except after a period of revolutionary change.

Russia's role in the creation of a new Balkan united front in 1912 aroused wide speculation. The tsar's foreign minister, A. P. Izvolsky (1906–1911), who had brought about a world-wide balance of interests in the agreement with Great Britain over Persia, Afghanistan and Tibet of August 18th–31st, 1907, had without a doubt tried to use Austria's isolated position in 1908 in order to receive compensation in respect of the clauses concerning the use of the Dardanelles. His diplomatic defeat during the annexation crisis had given great stimulus to the champions of a defensive Balkan policy whose chief aims were to curb Austrian expansion and fight the nationalism of the young Turks. More than once, close consideration had been given to the idea of bringing Turkey into a Balkan system of alliances. Unclear directives from the Russian government had been partly responsible for, and had also to a large extent provoked, the arbitrary attitudes and intrigues of the Russian representatives in south-eastern Europe–N. V. Charykov in Constantinople (from 1909 onwards), V. A. Neklindov in Sofia (from 1911 onwards), and N. G. Hartvig in Belgrade (1909–1914)–their intrigues often being directed against one another.

The Russian government therefore encouraged a balance of interests in the negotiations between the two main Balkan groups although she could not have a decisive influence in their final discussions, which concerned objectives and possible changes in their alliance system. Taking advantage of the Italian-Turkish war over Tripoli in September 1911, Serbia and Bulgaria proceeded to negotiate a treaty in March 1912 by which they agreed to a joint approach over the Balkan question. A Bulgarian-Greek treaty followed on May 29th, 1912. In September–October 1912, Montenegro gave her support as well, thereby not only providing the keystone to the Balkan alliance but also revealing its anti-Turkish bias.

King Nicholas of Montenegro's support for the rising in north Albania in 1911 had already brought him into confrontation with the Turks. On October 6th, he broke off diplomatic relations with them and two days later he declared war on the Porte, Serbia, Bulgaria and Greece joining him as allies on October 17th. The military outcome of the war was quickly decided. Within a few weeks, Ottoman supremacy in the Balkan peninsula had completely collapsed before the concentrated attack of the allied armies. The treaty of London of May 30th, 1913, which brought the 'first Balkan war' to its conclusion through pressure from the great powers, reduced Turkish possessions in Europe to a small strip of land outside Istanbul. However, the conflicting objectives of the Balkan countries that had been suppressed by necessity were now laid bare in the unmitigated violence that occurred in the sharing out of the booty. Once more the Macedonian problem proved to be the crux.

Bulgaria's attempt to achieve a fait accompli by a lightning military action was met with a counter-offensive by Serbia and Greece in which Montenegro, Romania and Turkey–still smarting from her defeat–took part. During this 'second Balkan war', which lasted from June 29th to August 10th, 1913, tsar Ferdinand was ultimately forced to abandon his dream of achieving Bulgarian supremacy in the Balkans. He was compelled by the treaty of Bucharest to make substantial territorial concessions. Southern Dobrudja fell to the Romanians; Turkey re-established her European outpost in Thrace and regained Adrianople (Edirne); most of Macedonia was divided up between Serbia and Greece, who acquired the Macedonian coast and its crucial port, Salonica. Only a narrow band of territory along the eastern border of Macedonia was conceded to Bulgaria.

But the provisions of the treaty of Bucharest did not bring the Balkan countries the peace they had been hoping for. In Bulgaria, demands for a revision of the harsh peace terms became vociferous; irredentists in Serbia urged their brothers under Habsburg rule to revolt; the independence of Albania was only to be achieved after massive intervention by the great powers. While the concept of a universal Ottoman empire was gradually being abandoned, the new Balkan countries did not themselves have the resources to build up an effective political structure to replace it. The Balkan wars were the symptoms of a profound internal crisis during the transition to a new period of Balkan history.

The turbulent years after the Bosnia crisis had helped Albania along the road to independence and self-government, which she was last of all the Balkan peoples to attain. The circumstances under which she had been incorporated into the Turkish empire had delayed Albania's birth of national consciousness. Furthermore, the fact that seventy per cent of her population were Muslims had made it easier for her to accept the Ottoman conception of empire. The Greek-inspired hierarchy of the Orthodox church which twenty per cent recognized—southern Albania being an important Orthodox area, while a Catholic minority consisting of about ten per cent of the population had maintained itself in north Albania—had not shown much interest in Albanian nationalist aspirations, either. It is understandable, then, that the first co-ordinated political activities with nationalist aims had to be stimulated from outside.

In 1878, Albanian nationalist leaders had set up in Prizren an 'Albanian league for the protection of the rights of the Albanian nation' as a defence against Montenegrin, Serbian, Bulgarian and Greek expansionism. At first, Albania could count on Turkish support in her resistance to Montenegrin claims to Podgorica and Antivari and Greek designs on areas in Epirus and Thessaly. But hopes for joining together the *vilayets* of Monastir, Yannina and Scutari, largely inhabited by Albanians, and granting them autonomy within the Turkish empire, were soon shattered. The Turkish authorities, who had not failed to notice the country's dangerous nationalistic tendencies, brought about the dissolution of the League in 1881.

Even so, these measures did not mean an end to nationalist

agitation, which received much encouragement from new ideas infiltrated through Albanian emigré centres in Italy and America. The Franciscan mission and the Jesuits among the northern Albanian Catholics had already made preparations for the building of national schools and for the formation of a graded system for Albanian education. In the matter of deciding on an Albanian alphabet as the first step in the creation of an Albanian literature, the Latin faction won a victory over the Muslim one, which was in favour of using the Arabic script. Nevertheless, the realization of national aspirations within the Ottoman empire was preferred to more radical solutions until the revolutionary efforts of the young Turks to promote a strong central, Islamic government threatened the provincial autonomy that the Albanians had won. From the beginning of 1909 onwards, unrest, risings and guerrilla warfare continued ceaselessly in Albanian territory, and they were to give the neighbouring states their desired pretext for diplomatic and military intervention.

In 1912, king Nicholas of Montenegro finally took advantage of events in Albania and declared war on the Porte, as we have just seen, the countries united in the 'Balkan alliance' joining forces with him. The outcome of the war, however, although it was in the allies' favour, left little scope for the establishment of an Albanian national state. Only energetic remonstrations on the part of Austria and Italy prevented a sharing out of Albanian territory in which the lion's share would have gone to Serbia.

The open policy of obstruction pursued by her neighbours was largely responsible for the general failure to find a lasting solution to the Albanian question in the few months before the outbreak of the first world war. The international conference of foreign ministers which was to determine the country's frontiers proved unequal to the task. The German prince Wilhelm zu Wied who was elected ruler of Albania was to leave in 1914 after six months there, as he found the internal political situation too difficult to deal with. Although the national leaders Ismail Kemal Bey Vlora and Essad Pasha submitted to the International Control Commission and put aside their claims, the German prince–who was unfamiliar with Albania–was unable to bring about any lasting reconciliation of differences or to establish an effective central government. The disputes over the creation of an Albanian state were basically no more than a part of the overall Balkan crisis whose resolution appeared more and more to depend on radical measures.

Serbia had considered herself cheated of the fruits of her glorious victory of 1913 by the intervention of Austria-Hungary, and she had therefore begun to oppose this multi-national state that controlled large areas she claimed for herself, and that had seemed so unfortunate in its policy towards the various nationalities it encompassed. Serbian nationalism found it could no longer put up with the annexation of Bosnia and Herzegovina. The federal reconstruction of the Danube monarchy had come to a standstill in mid-stream after the settlement with Hungary in 1867, as has been described, so that the southern Slav and Romanian populations in Croatia, Slavonia, the Vojvodina and Transylvania had seen themselves confronted with a Hungarian nation whose undisguised determination to impose its will had not been effectively curbed by the settlement with Croatia in 1868.

A rational approach making for a tripartite solution to the problem of the national groups became impossible because of the growing tension between Serbia and Austria caused by the explosive concept of 'Yugoslavia', which aimed at the destruction of the Habsburg monarchy and the creation of an all-embracing Slav state. The clash between the idea of a southern Slav federation and 'greater Serbian' nationalism had reached dangerous proportions by the beginning of the twentieth century, and it provided the material for a conflagration. When this eventually came as a result of the Sarajevo assassination, the mechanics of the European system of alliances allowed the Balkan origins of the crisis to be forgotten, and drew the nations of Europe into a world-wide military conflict.

The assassination by a young Bosnian nationalist, Gavrilo Princip, of archduke Franz Ferdinand, the successor to the Austrian throne, on June 28th, 1914, was engineered by a group of conspirators called the 'Ujedinjenje ili Smrt' (meaning 'unity or death'), who were better known as the 'Black Hand'. Some years

Map 10. The Balkans and the Austro-Hungarian empire, 1914

before, they had decided that terrorism was the best means of realizing their revolutionary pan-Serbian aims. The archduke, who had supported the reconstruction of the Danube monarchy on a tripartite basis and the negotiation of a settlement with the Yugoslav nationalists on the lines of that of 1867, had been the hope of the moderates. The scant agreement between the Black Hand's objectives and the radical 'greater Serbian' programme of Pašić, the prime minister, had not been conducive to close co-operation. Nevertheless, some links between them did exist, despite the absence of official contact. The question whether the Serbian government was in reality directly–or at any rate morally–implicated in the assassination has often been posed. However, the events of the war made it irrelevant, and in the trials that took place subsequently it was never ultimately cleared up.

A genuine willingness to achieve a peaceful settlement was lacking on all sides after June 28th. In Vienna, the war party which had formed round the foreign minister, count von Berchtold, and the chief of general staff, general F. Conrad von Hötzendorf, gained the upper hand over the voices of caution. The ultimatum given to Serbia on July 23rd had not been expected to meet with acceptance, but it was Russia's over-hasty movement of troops after the Austro-Hungarian declaration of war on July 28th that now made it impossible to contain the conflict. Declarations of war by the other European countries, who were bound by reciprocal treaties, followed in rapid succession.

The outbreak of war took the Balkan countries by surprise, engrossed as they were in their internal dissensions. Serbia's army, which had but recently withstood an offensive on the part of Austro-Hungarian troops in 1914, and was preparing a counter-offensive, was to collapse completely under the concentrated attack of its hostile neighbours, Turkey having entered the war on the side of the central European powers in 1914, and Bulgaria in September 1915. At the beginning of 1916, king Peter of Serbia was able to save some of his troops by evacuating them to the island of Corfu after a legendary retreat to the Adriatic coast, but a desperate attempt to bring help made by the allies, who had just conducted an unsuccessful campaign in the Dardanelles, landing at Gallipoli in April 1915, had failed because of the strict neutrality observed by Greece. Out of loyalty to his royal brother-in-law in Berlin, king Constantine of Greece had ignored the remonstrances of Venizelos, his prime minister, who had known that the majority of people in the country had been behind him, and had in 1915 taken it upon himself to allow the allied troops to land in Salonica. It was only after Constantine's forced abdication in June 1917 that the war in south-eastern Europe was to take a turn for the better. In an allied counter-offensive conducted from Salonica in September 1918, the positions of the central European powers were overrun, Bulgaria concluding a separate peace treaty as early as September 29th, 1918, and so opting out of a war which had become hopeless for her. Serbian military contingents now took over the task of liberating their country: on October 12th they succeeded in taking Niš, and on November 1st, 1918, they entered the capital, Belgrade. The Italian front had already collapsed at the end of October.

The defeat of Austria-Hungary was followed by a general breakaway movement on the part of the Balkan nationals, who severed their long-standing ties with the Habsburgs. The emperor Charles's famous manifesto of October 16th, 1918, which converted the Danube monarchy into a federal state, and attempted to forestall the independence movements, came too late. For on October 29th, 1918, the Sabor in Zagreb proclaimed the secession of Croatia, Slavonia and Dalmatia. The national assemblies of Slovenia and Bosnia-Herzegovina swiftly followed suit.

The withdrawal of Russia and Turkey, too, from participation in Balkan affairs—Russia having undergone the October revolution in 1917, and Turkey having been defeated in the war—gave the nations of south-eastern Europe their first chance to take their future into their hands for over five hundred years. The last phase in the creation of the new states was concluded by the peace treaties that were signed in various suburbs of Paris (as distinct from the treaty of Versailles). They were negotiated under the banner of the principle of national self-determination proclaimed by president Wilson in his Fourteen Points of January 8th, 1918. These treaties were, however, to be chiefly responsible for the international tensions and internal difficulties encountered in the consolidation of the new states during the next few decades. It was because when the new frontiers were drawn up, concessions were made to the aspirations of the victorious Balkan countries, allowing them to establish their own national 'empires'.

Bulgaria suffered less, in her lone Balkan defeat, through her relatively small territorial losses than through the substantial reparations and restrictions that were imposed on her such as excessively high financial payments, limitations on her military strength and prevention of access to the Aegean. By the treaty of Neuilly of November 27th, 1919, she was obliged to restore the Dobrudja to her Romanian neighbour, cede western Thrace to Greece and suffer frontier adjustments in favour of Yugoslavia on strategic grounds. Tsar Ferdinand, who had been unlucky in the Balkan wars, had, in spite of his many hesitations, backed the wrong horse once more in the first world war. He had had to pay the penalty. In face of growing dissatisfaction in the countryside where the peasant leader, Alexander Stambulijski, released from prison, had proclaimed a short-lived republic, he had abdicated in favour of his son, Boris–to become Boris III–on October 4th, 1918. Although Stambulijski had gained a resounding victory in the elections of April 1919, even he had been unable as leader of the Bulgarian delegation at the Paris Peace Conference to circumvent the territorial claims which had been made on Bulgaria.

The British, French, United States and Italian delegates had shown themselves unwilling to respond to appeals for national self-determination when faced with contentious situations. Active resistance proved to be the only means of obtaining concessions from the 'big four'. It was in this way that Turkey was in the end able, in spite of her military defeat, to secure the revision of some important provisions in the treaty of Sèvres of August 10th, 1920, by the treaty of Lausanne of July 23rd, 1923. This followed Kemal Atatürk's revolution and the successful resistance Turkey put up against the Greek offensive in Smyrna (Izmir). Nevertheless, she had to reconcile herself to the ending of her dominant position in the Balkans and to the loss of her provinces in south-eastern Europe.

Among the profoundest changes in the political map brought about by the Paris treaties were the complete disruption of Hungary's boundaries, the formation of a federal state that included the Serbs, Croats and Slovenes, and the creation of a greater Romania. By the treaty of Trianon of June 4th, 1920, Hungary was left with a bare third of her former territory. The historic provinces of upper Hungary, Slovakia and Ruthenia, together with the important towns of Pressburg (Bratislava), Kaschau (Košice) and Munkacs (Mukachevo), were attached to the newly created state of Czechoslovakia. Yugoslavia acquired the southern Hungarian territories of Baranja, Bačka and Banat, which were incorporated into the Vojvodina. The contested territories of Transylvania, Bukovina (including the town of Czernowitz (Chernovtsy)) and the Banat of Temesvár (Timişoara) were given to Romania, who more than doubled her territory. Thanks to the skilful and purposeful diplomacy of Ionel Brătianu, Romania had come close to realizing her ancient dream of a national empire—though it was at the cost of creating a minority problem that was to jeopardize her internal consolidation.

All these territorial changes were no more approved by true plebiscites than was the problematical demarcation of the north and north-west frontiers of the newly created kingdom of Yugoslavia. With a view to securing her entry into the war, the allies had agreed to substantial territorial acquisitions by Italy, who had till then remained neutral, in the treaty of London of April 26th, 1915. The Italian insistence on the honouring of these obligations was nearly to disrupt the Paris Peace Conference. The cession of the South Tyrol up to the Brenner pass could be imposed on what remained of the Austrian state, and justified by a manipulation of ethnographic maps. Satisfaction, however, of the Italian claims to Istria and the Dalmatian coast involved not merely a denial of the indigenous Slav population's right to self-determination but also an affront to the Serbs who were their allies. The resulting quarrel was not provisionally shelved until five years later. By the treaty between Italy and Yugoslavia of January 27th, 1924, Fiume (or Rijeka), which had been occupied on September 12th, 1919, by Gabriele D'Annunzio and his volunteers in a sensational surprise move, was given to Italy without any hinterland–the suburb of Sušak remaining in Yugoslav hands–together with the seaport of Trieste and Istria; while Yugoslavia finally obtained the Dalmatian coast with the exception of the islands of Chesso (Cres), Lussino (Lošinj) and Lagosta (Lastovo) and the Dalmatian capital, Zara (Zadar), which all remained with Italy. Yugoslavia also extended her northern territory far into the area with a mixed Slovenian and German population, Austria having to cede Kranj together with the city of Ljubljana as well as lower Styria with Maribor, Ptuj and Celje. On the other hand, her push towards southern Carinthia and Klagenfurt was successfully resisted, and in that area only Dravograd and the Mistal were lost to Austria.

The former southern Slav subjects of the Danube monarchy in 1918 decided in favour of joining with the Serbs to make the 'Kingdom of Serbs, Croats and Slovenes', or the S.H.S., which stands for 'Kraljevina Srba, Hrvata i Slovenaca', Montenegro announcing her accession after the forced abdication of king Nicholas at Podgorica (Titograd). The act of union was officially celebrated on December 1st, 1918, in Belgrade. A delegation of the Croatian national assembly in Zagreb under the leadership of Svetozar Pribičević conveyed to king Alexander, the Serbian successor to the throne, a formal address which, in accordance with previous agreements, was followed by a solemn proclamation of the union. This late realization of the southern Slav concept of unity resulted from a compromise between two forces. On the one hand, there had been the movement for a 'greater Serbia' that had accepted the ideas of centralization and annexation and found its expression in the radical party of Pašić, obtaining strong support from the officers' corps and the court of Belgrade; and on the other, there had been the ideals of the southern Slavs of the Habsburg empire who had looked more for a federal balance between the different sections of the population. The spirit of compromise had found public expression in the famous 'Declaration of Corfu' of July 20th, 1917, in which Pašić and the president of the 'Yugoslav Committee' (the Jugoslovenski Odbor) in London, Ante Trumbić, had agreed on principles for the future political organization of the southern Slav peoples: there was to be full equality among the three nation states, the Slovenes, the Croats and the Serbs, in political, religious and cultural matters–equal recognition being given to the Catholic, Orthodox and Muslim religions, and to the Latin and Cyrillic alphabets–under the constitutional monarchy of the Karadjordjević family. The 'spirit of Corfu', to which the Serbian government had professed its adherence in view of the events of the war and of its successful evacuation under dramatic circumstances, was to be subjected to its greatest test in the period between the two wars.

THE EFFECTS OF THE TREATY
OF VERSAILLES

The break-up of the Habsburg monarchy and the Ottoman empire into a number of small independent states by no means signified victory for the new principle of the nation state over multi-national ideals in the Balkans. Romania and the kingdom of Yugoslavia, in particular, with their large minorities were distinctly multi-national. People of fifteen different nationalities and ethnic groups lived together on Yugoslav territory, while Romania had minorities amounting to twenty-seven per cent of her total population and encompassing nineteen nationalities.

Every effort was made to ease internal tension by liberal policies towards all the groups. It was difficult, however, to preserve the laboriously achieved balances in relations between the states. For the bilateral pacts designed to prevent irredentist movements, which were almost exclusively directed against the 'losers' in the first world war, Hungary and Bulgaria, greatly intensified the atmosphere of mistrust, and led to perilous juggling with alliances and to secret agreements.

It had been in the last phase of the Paris Peace Conference that French diplomacy had encouraged and promoted bilateral defensive alliances between the nations who had succeeded the former Austro-Hungarian Danube monarchy, partly to protect them against Hungarian revisionism, and partly to secure France's supremacy in central Europe. On August 14th, 1920, Czechoslovakia and the kingdom of Yugoslavia had organized a meeting in Belgrade where a treaty had been signed that was to become the model for a number of other treaties such as, for instance, the military pact between Romania and Czechoslovakia of April 23rd, 1921, and the treaty between Romania and Yugoslavia of June 7th that year. The participation of France in the system was exemplified by the treaties she made with Poland on February 19th, 1921, Czechoslovakia on January 25th, 1924, and later Romania in 1926 and Yugoslavia in 1927. Although there were many attempts to provide a broader foundation for these treaties and to build up a politically united Balkan front from the existing community of economic interests among the agrarian states, and in the early 1930s, during the world economic crisis, they held a series of conferences in Athens, Istanbul, Bucharest and Salonica on the initiative of the Greeks, the basis for closer collaboration–in the form of a non-aggression pact and the provision of guarantees for the status quo in inter-state relations–failed to materialize because Bulgaria contested the validity of the agreements signed at Neuilly. The Balkan pact of February 1934 between Greece, Yugoslavia, Romania and Turkey, which was regarded as both a last resort and a first step in a new direction, could do no more than consolidate the existing alignments between the Balkan states.

It was inevitable that Hungary, Bulgaria and Albania should see the system of alliances formed in the 1920s–the 'Little Entente' –and the Balkan pact as direct threats. They therefore sought to overcome their isolation by looking for strong partners for a defensive alliance, a circumstance that favoured Mussolini's active policy in the Balkans. Mussolini proceeded to create friendly ties with revisionist elements in Hungary and Bulgaria, establish links with independence movements among the Croatians, and build up Albania as his Italian bridgehead on the Balkan peninsula. The desperate efforts to achieve a broadly based balance of interests among all the states on the eve of the second world war came too late. South-eastern Europe entered the war politically divided and paid a high price in murderous fratricidal strife for the failures of the inter-war years. Special circumstances within individual states had been a contributory factor.

Internally, the states had obviously not kept up with the general growth in political independence resulting from the nineteenth-century national liberation movements. The mainly agricultural structure of their societies had failed to produce either an effective class of leaders or a continuous political tradition capable of containing their centrifugal forces. Since the establishment of

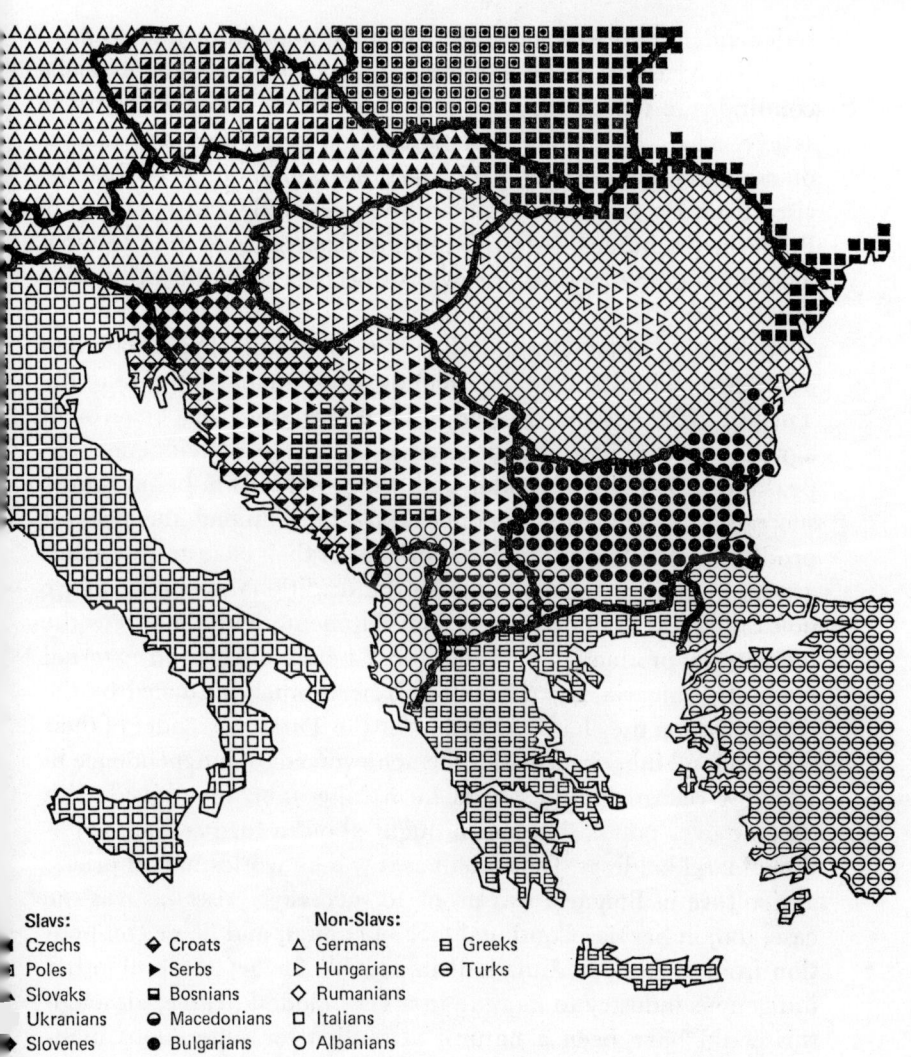

Slavs:

			Non-Slavs:		
◀	Czechs	◆ Croats	△	Germans	⊟ Greeks
◢	Poles	▶ Serbs	▷	Hungarians	⊖ Turks
▲	Slovaks	▣ Bosnians	◇	Rumanians	
	Ukranians	◕ Macedonians	☐	Italians	
◆	Slovenes	● Bulgarians	○	Albanians	

Map 11. Races in the Balkans, 1918

independent Balkan states after 1878, their population had doubled in thirty years, thereby causing a severe deterioration in social conditions in the countryside and a land hunger that was hard to satisfy. The consequence was pressure on prices and dependence on creditors. Between 1878 and 1914, the population of Serbia had risen from 1·7 to 3·02 million, and between 1881 and 1911 that of Bulgaria (including eastern Rumelia) from 2·82 to 4·33 million, Thorough-going land reform was to become a matter of life and death.

In Serbia, Miloš Obrenović (1817–1839 and 1859–1860) had done away with the feudal agricultural system and the evils of the Turkish *čifluk* system of land inheritance, and his benevolent agrarian policy had aimed at creating a free and independent peasantry. But lack of capital had prevented it from being totally successful. Absence of economic know-how among the peasant producers, who had the limited horizons of their class and were but gradually freeing themselves from the traditional social structure holding back their economic development, had debarred the increase in productivity needed for a better balance in external trade. In Bulgaria, the peasants had been much burdened by the compensation they had had to pay for the Turks' surrender of their right to land inheritance after the achievement of independence in 1878. A reform in the law of farm inheritance combined with chronic over-population had brought about a further fragmentation of land holdings. Dependent as it was on world-market prices, agriculture in Bulgaria was prone to successive crises – as was the case, too, in Serbia. Continual lack of capital, and fierce competition from abroad, had made it impossible for her to develop her indigenous industry to more than a very modest degree, although this could have been a natural attraction for superfluous manpower on the land. As elsewhere in the Balkans, the result was growing foreign indebtedness and economic dependence. Even Yugoslavia, a country with rich mineral resources where there was considerable foreign capital investment, drew only a relatively small part of her national income from their exploitation in 1939.

The regions that had belonged to the Habsburg empire could look forward to better economic conditions. As part of a large-scale economic unit, they had already been through the necessary processes of social change. In the kingdom of Yugoslavia, these processes had been accelerated by the dissolution of the old social order and the breaking up of the big estates that had begun with the first land reform enactment of February 25th, 1919, and they had brought the politically mature class of former big landowners to prominence in the government. The same thing had happened in Bosnia and Herzegovina as well. Under the intense pressures of class interest, well-meaning attempts at reform had in the end been deflected from their original purpose. Above all in Bosnia, Herzegovina and south Albania, the overwhelming mass of the agricultural population was to remain dependent on a numerically small and, generally speaking, Muslim upper class even after the break-up of the Danube monarchy.

Individual territories made very uneven economic development, which had rendered integration difficult; and this, coupled with political, cultural and religious conflict, had provided tinder for the disputes to come. At the beginning of the twentieth century, seventy-nine per cent of the population in Yugoslavia (it was still only seventy-five per cent in 1938) and eighty per cent in Bulgaria lived on the land in what were often intolerable conditions. Nevertheless, the people on the land only took part in parliamentary struggles intermittently or in a regional context as a group conscious of its class background. Although peasant parties were formed in all the Balkan states, it was not except in Romania —with the 'Tsaranists' under Ion Mihalache and Iulius Maniu— and among the Croatians where Stjepan Radić was the peasant leader that they had a lasting influence in internal politics. In Bulgaria, Alexander Stambulijski started an extensive programme of reform which was to improve agricultural conditions by the redistribution of land on the basis of the law of 1920. But while trying to bring about an understanding with Yugoslavia he was attacked by nationalist and reactionary circles, and after the military coup d'état of June 9th, 1923, he was brutally murdered by fanatical members of the I.M.R.O. With his death, the Agrarians lost their decisive role and disappeared from politics, having been responsible for the government for exactly five years.

Stjepan Radić also met with a violent death in the 1920s. On June 20th, 1928, he was shot by a Montenegrin extremist of the radical party with a revolver in the Skupština (the parliament) and severely wounded, dying a few days later. The Croatian peasant movement that had originally represented agrarian class interests had by this time become nation-wide, working for autonomy against Serbian aspirations for a centralized and unitary state. His successor to the party leadership, Dr. Vladimir Maček, was to demand a federal reform of the Yugoslav constitution. The demand was met in January 1929 by king Alexander (1921–1934) who suspended the constitution of 1921, the Vidovdan constitution, and established a royal dictatorship. This unusual turn of events foreshadowed other constitutional developments in the Balkans in the period between the wars.

Though parliamentary government had been introduced from outside during the nineteenth century, it was a system that had been foreign to the realities of south-eastern Europe. The great powers, always ready to intervene, had planned to counterbalance the strength of foreign princes summoned to Balkan thrones and of local leaders with strong parliamentary systems. The model of the Belgian constitution–which had been established in exemplary fashion on the principle of the sovereignty of the people–had made a firm impression on the Balkan intelligentsia educated in the west, and was a decisive influence in all constitutional discussions in the Balkans. However, in actual practice a constitution based on such republican and constitutional ideas was to have a corrupting effect. Balkan parliamentary life was the main concern of a small upper class. This class had lost its professional ties and had turned into a new oligarchy that used the parliamentary machine for its own profit and for the achievement of its own selfish aims. True democracy was denied the masses because they had been hostile for centuries to the idea of state authority and because they lacked the necessary educational background: in 1921 51·5 per cent of the Yugoslav population was illiterate–though there were considerable regional differences in the percentage, so that in Slovenia it was 8·8 per cent while in Macedonia it was 83·8 per cent. In the Balkan countries, then, there was neither any real opposition to the power of the state nor a politically mature and organized society to act as a counterweight in internal conflicts of interest. Nor was there any effective control over the legislature and executive.

The parliamentary system was to show signs of serious disorder in all the states. Behind the constitutional disputes of the nineteenth and twentieth centuries in Serbia, Bulgaria, Greece and Romania, there were irreconcilable antagonisms that were not so much between the power of the princes and the parliamentary system as between different sections of the oligarchy with whom the royal houses were inextricably involved.

The constitutional development in Serbia was typical. In 1838, Miloš Obrenović had found his autocratic way of government curtailed by the sultan's intervention. A year later, he had been forced to abdicate by oligarchic forces in the senate–the constitution of 1838 having provided for the creation of a council of seventeen senators who had a predominant position. A fatal illness had prevented his elder son, Milan, from succeeding to the throne. After three years, his second son Michael was to come into conflict with the regency, which had the support of the senate. Alexander Karadjordjević (1842–1858), the son of the legendary Karadjordje, who succeeded him, had then ruled as mouthpiece of the senate, not allowing the Skupština any significant influence in the government. This body had only met again in 1858–to bring the now ageing Miloš Obrenović back to the throne. In 1861, Michael (1860–1868), his successor, had introduced a constitution which left him more or less free to carry out his progressive Balkan policies. Michael's murder in 1868 had then led to a return to oligarchy under the 'Whitsun constitution' of the regency, which had finally been superseded by a parliamentary system with the constitutions of 1888 and 1903. However, this system was to be increasingly overshadowed by the dominating figure of Nikola Pašić: the centralizing tendencies of his radical party were to leave a decisive imprint on the constitution of the new kingdom of Yugoslavia in 1921 and outweigh the concessions made to Croatian federalism in the declaration of Corfu.

In Bulgaria, the penetration of liberal ideas had been furthered by active Russian influence. The so-called Trnovo constitution of April 1878 with its single-chamber system and its recognition of the principle of ministerial responsibility must be considered one of the most progressive constitutional documents in south-east European history, although in practice the agrarian society of Bulgaria was unable to support a parliamentary system of government. Alexander von Battenberg sought in vain to get round the restrictive provisions of the constitution in 1881 to 1883; under the authoritarian régime of Stambulov, the young Ferdinand was in danger of being deprived of any political responsibility. Ferdinand was in fact able to rid himself of his inconvenient partner in 1894, as we saw in chapter 9, but because of his unfortunate foreign policy he was to lose his throne. Under his successor, Boris III, the terrorist tactics of the I.M.R.O. dominated the political scene more and more after Stambulijski's peasant party and the communists—who were strongly represented in the parliament—had been pushed underground in the period following the coup d'état of 1923. The country was to reach the verge of civil war. The only way out of the situation was again a royal dictatorship. The officer's coup of May 19th, 1934, led by colonel Damian Velčev and the transitional government of Kimon Georgiev (1934–1935) that made an important contribution to the restoration of peace in its disbanding of the I.M.R.O. organization and its progressive policies for the peasants, had prepared the way for the king's intervention. Boris was merely to use the officers who were loyal to the crown as tools for winning back his former influence on the government, and by removing the army from politics he was able to conduct a personal system of rule based on chosen men of confidence right up to his death on August 23rd, 1943.

Such a system was copied by the neighbouring state of Romania. King Carol, excluded from the succession because of his liaison with Madame Lupescu, had left the country in 1923. After his return in 1930 as Carol II (1930–1940), he had managed first to manoeuvre himself into a dominating political position and then to bring the government under his control with the new Romanian constitution of 1938, over-ruling all existing parliamentary institutions.

In Greece, on the other hand, the military coup d'état of 1935 and the overthrow of the republic that had been created by the plebiscite of April 13th, 1924, led not to the restoration of the monarchy of George II but to the dictatorship of general Metaxas. Although he only voiced the opinions of a small extreme right-wing group, he was able to maintain himself in power from 1936 until 1941, the year of his death.

Contrary to what the great powers might have hoped for, the constitution in Albania was never to recognize a division of function between the sovereign monarch and the controlling parliamentary institutions. The irreconcilable social tensions between the big landowners, who were mostly of the Muslim faith, and the mass of the population complicated the work of reconstruction in this troubled land. It was with extreme difficulty that national self-determination was achieved in the turbulent years of the first world war and post-war period. During the war, Albania lost her frontier territories to Montenegro, Serbia–whose military units were later disbanded by the Austrians–and Greece. By landing near Valona in October 1914, the Italians had secured for themselves a vantage point for the protection of their own interests, and with the collapse of the central European powers, Italian troops were to be found next to French and Serbian contingents among the occupation forces in the greater part of the country. But for president Wilson's unyielding determination and the skilful tactics of the Albanian representative at the Paris Peace Conference, there would have been a joint action by Italy and Greece to carve up Albania in accordance with the agreement between Venizelos and Tittoni of July 29th, 1919, and the Anglo-French proposal to intervene in support of Yugoslav territorial acquisitions in north Albania would have been accepted. The complete withdrawal of the Italians from Albania was achieved by a national rising in May 1920.

Two social factions confronted one another uncompromisingly in Albania's burning internal disputes: the Muslim 'Progressive Party' under the leadership of Shefqet Vërlaci, and the progressive forces favouring reform round the Orthodox bishop Fan S. Noli, who had returned from exile in America and could count on strong backing from the land-hungry peasantry in south Albania. In marrying the daughter of Shefqet Vërlaci, the unscrupulous and ambitious Ahmed Zog was to switch his support from the reform movement to conservative class interests. The discontent in the country which brought Fan Noli temporarily to the head of the government forced Zog to flee to Belgrade. However, a few months later, with support from the Yugoslavs–and also from the remnants of the White Russian Wrangel army–Zog recrossed the Albanian frontier on December 13th, 1924, and took over control of the state. The national assembly elected him president on January 31st, 1925. By means of the constitution of March 7th, 1925, ensuring his personal power, and financial support from the Italians, he reinforced his position further, and on December 1st, 1928, he gave it the stamp of glory by assuming the title of king.

An Italian financial group had established the National Bank of Albania and assumed control of the Albanian economy, so that it was difficult for Zog to offset the consequences of the Tirana agreement of November 27th, 1927, imposed by the Italians and steer an independent course between them and the Yugoslavs. In the decisive phase of the conflict in the thirties he could not count either on the necessary backing from his own people or on support from outside in resisting Italy's demands, which were put in the form of an ultimatum. On April 8th, 1939, after Italian troops had landed and entered Tirana, king Zog I retired to Greece.

With the Italian invasion of Albania on the eve of the second world war, the Balkan peninsula had fallen again under the influence of foreign powers, who had found a suitable climate for agitation in the disunity and economic and political weakness of its states. Hitler's policy of expansion had made itself felt to the east and south-east through the 1938 Anschluss with Austria and the annexation of Czechoslovakia in 1938–1939, and had loosened the links between France and the members of the Little Entente, for the strength of the German economy had brought the latter into greater economic dependence. In 1938, for example, the German Reich had been responsible for 63·6 per cent of Bulgaria's exports and 57·9 per cent of her imports, for 50 per cent of Yugoslavia's exports and imports, and for 35·9 per cent of Romania's exports and 48·5 per cent of her imports. At the same time, debts to English, Belgian and French creditors had been made good by loans of German capital.

The growing threat from Germany and Italy and the knowledge that France and the League of Nations could no longer guarantee the integrity of the states had led individual governments to retreat from their military obligations under the treaties of the Little Entente. In Romania, the replacement of N. Titulescu as foreign minister by Victor Antonescu in 1936 meant a reversal of the country's rigidly hostile policy towards Germany and a simultaneous rapprochement with Poland. In Yugoslavia, Stojadinović had negotiated a pact of friendship with Bulgaria, who had for a long time been considered outside the pale, and had concluded in March 1937 a non-aggression pact with Mussolini that had caused a considerable stir. In this, he had not only obtained favourable economic terms but also an important commitment from the Italian government to withdraw its support for the terrorist Ustaša movement in Croatia. It was a desperate effort to meet the need for national security by denouncing the system of collective security, which was still a mere fiction, and resorting to bilateral agreements. But very few of these agreements stood the test during the second world war.

Hitler's unexpectedly swift military success against Poland and France caused the Soviet Union to issue an ultimatum to Romania for the surrender of Bessarabia, which had been promised her by Hitler in a secret protocol attached to the German non-aggression pact of August, 1939. Germany and Italy advised Romania to comply with the ultimatum, and proceeded to give recognition to Hungarian and Bulgarian territorial claims on Transylvania and south Dobrudja in the so-called 'second Vienna arbitration' of August 30th, 1940, and treaty of Craiova of September 7th, 1940, without consulting the Soviet government. King Carol was forced to bow to the national outcry in his country and abdicate in favour of his son, Michael in September 1940. By attacking Romania's previous policy of adherence to the Balkan alliance and turning to the Axis powers, the authoritarian régime of general Ion Antonescu was at least able to obtain guarantees for what remained of the country's much reduced territory. The sending of German military instructors to Romania was to arouse the suspicions of Moscow over the growing influence of Hitler in south-eastern Europe; it also made Mussolini realize—as he anticipated the military conflict with the Soviet Union which had by then been decided upon—that he was condemned to carry through his threatened attack on Greece (war having been declared with her on October 28th, 1940) in order to build up his bridgehead in Albania. The unexpected defeat of the aggressor in the memorable defensive battle of Metsovo on November 11th, 1940, and the Greek counter-attack on Albanian territory brought about the intervention of Germany. South-eastern Europe had become the battleground of more foreign powers.

Within a few weeks preparations had been made. Bulgaria, who was closely linked with the Axis powers, gave her agreement to the transit of German forces from Romania in January 1941. Then, following the example of Hungary and Romania (November 1940), she pronounced her support for the three-power pact between Germany, Italy and Japan on March 1st, 1941. On March 25th, the Yugoslav government gave way to massive German pressure and agreed to sign a treaty that, in return for an assurance of Yugoslav neutrality, promised to exempt Yugoslav territory from German troop movements and offered it the hope of acquiring Salonica. The country in general, however, did not wish to honour the agreement made by the Cvetković government. A military coup in Belgrade on March 27th was to bring about a surprising reversal of the situation. Prince Paul, who had been regent since 1934, resigned, and Peter, who was still a minor, ascended the Yugoslav throne as king Peter II. A new government under general Dušan Simović took over the leadership and cautiously attempted to adopt a neutral stance between the power blocks. But on the morning of April 6th, Germany countered with a devastating air attack on Belgrade, and in a blitzkrieg lasting a few weeks crushed Yugoslav and Greek resistance. Belgrade fell on April 12th, 1941, and Athens on April 27th. For the next four years—until the end of 1944—the Balkans were to be forcibly united under a single rule.

The German military administration together with the allied governments of Italy, Bulgaria, Romania and Hungary naturally provided new encouragement for the revisionist and separatist tendencies that had been suppressed in the period between the wars. Another large-scale territorial readjustment took place, and the Paris peace arrangements were revised according to the wishes of the nations that had been defeated in 1918. Bulgaria now saw her old claims in Macedonia satisfied; Hungary regained her southern territories of Baranja and Bačka which she had lost in 1919 by the treaty of Trianon. In the north-west a compromise had to be made between the claims of Germany and Italy. Germany claimed lower Styria and parts of Kranj from Slovenia. Italy occupied Ljubljana, the Dalmatian ports of the Adriatic coast, the majority of the adjacant islands, excluding Pag, Brač and Hvar, and a part of Bosnia and Herzegovina. In addition, she kept Albania and exercised a protectorate over Montenegro.

One of the most damaging features of the policy of the German national socialist party in Yugoslavia was the bias it showed in the Croats' favour. The decision made in April 1941 to establish an independent Croatia had been certain to meet with agreement among the people of the country, since relations between Serbs and Croats had reached breaking point. After the collapse of the Danube monarchy at the end of the first world war, the original willingness of the Croats to enter into close union with their Serbian brothers in the spirit of the Corfu declaration had rapidly begun to wane. The reason was the abandonment of the compromise reached at Corfu between the programme of the prime minister Pašić for a greater Serbia and the Croatian idea of a southern Slav federation when the Croats had been faced with the political reality of Belgrade's centralizing policies. The Serbs as the true representatives of the nation had held the key positions in the cabinets that had followed one another in quick succession. The Vidovdan constitution of June 28th, 1921, had been only too clearly of Pašić's making and had been rejected outright by the Croatian representatives—in particular the peasant party of the brothers Antun (d. 1919) and Stjepan Radić. The boycotting of parliament, police intervention and a temporary coalition government of Pašić and Radić in 1925 had been different consequences of the bitter disagreement between the Croats and the Serbs, which had reached its peak with the murder of Radić in the Belgrade Skupština in 1928.

Confronted by this impasse and threatened with encirclement by Italy and her allies–Hungary, Albania and Bulgaria–king Alexander had agreed to a policy of centralization in the interests of the unity of the state, as mentioned. Radić's successor, Dr. Vladimir Maček, had been arrested. The new state, now officially called Yugoslavia, was divided into nine 'banats', with a prefecture in Belgrade, the boundaries imposed taking no account of the regions' historical backgrounds. Such an arrangement had obviously favoured the Serbian population because of the administrative separation of the areas inhabited by the Croats, and, under pressure from anti-Serbian emigrés, Croatian politicians had been more and more compelled to take up radical positions in the years following. The organization of the right-wing deputy, Dr. Ante Pavelić, which had first been called 'Domobran' and later 'Ustaša', had joined forces with the Bulgarian I.M.R.O. organization against the existing structure of the state. Early attempts at revolt in Croatia had been suppressed by force. Acts of violence on both sides had become more and more terrible. On October 9th, 1934, king Alexander had been murdered by Croatian and Bulgarian terrorists in Marseilles during a state visit to France, along with his host the French foreign minister Barthou. This senseless crime did exceptional damage to the Croatian cause both within the country and abroad. Faced by growing international tension and menacing developments on the Yugoslav frontiers in the north and north-west, the regent, prince Paul, had dismissed Stojadinović's government and opened the way for a reconciliation between Croats and Serbs. On August 25th, 1939, after several weeks of negotiations, the premier Cvetković and Dr. Maček had agreed on a federal reconstruction of the kingdom of Yugoslavia and on autonomy for the Croats in their famous pact, the *sporazum*, Maček entering the cabinet with five Croatian ministers. But the outbreak of the second world war was shortly to destroy any prospects of close collaboration between them.

Mussolini had been counting for some time on the Ustaša movement of Pavelić–who was now living in Italy–for the realization of his dreams of expansion in Dalmatia. As Maček had refused to collaborate with the national socialists, Hitler in the end raised no objections when on April 10th, 1941, Slavko Kvaternik proclaimed an independent state of Croatia in Zagreb in the name of Pavelić. On April 15th, Pavelić took over the position of leader or *poglavnik* in the Zagreb government. This government, however, was from the beginning greatly handicapped in the eyes of the people by its surrender of territories to Italy. Any resistance to it amongst the Croats was suppressed by force. Because of its wanton persecution of Jews and Serbs, the Ustaša state has left bloody memories: the partisan war waged by the opposition with unexampled savagery has an equally grim reputation.

Under the special conditions created by the German occupation, then, south-eastern Europe was to become the arena for a ruthless partisan war, for fratricide and for self-destruction. In the course of this war, new forces ultimately emerged which were destined to play a decisive role in the construction of a fresh political order after the withdrawal of German troops.

FROM NATIONAL TO SOCIAL
REVOLUTION

Partisan activity began very early during the German occupation of the defeated and fragmented state of Yugoslavia. Volunteers
inspired by patriotic sentiments and large sections of the regular
army united in opposition to foreign domination after the deliberate disbandment of the underground forces. Profound differences
of opinion concerning the immediate and long-term objectives of
the resistance movement were to produce many rival groupings.
The Chetnik (*četnici*) groups formed by the Yugoslav general
Draža Mihajlović became the focal point in west Serbia for the
resistance fighters who were in favour of a royalist 'greater Serbia'.
Mihajlović was the minister of war in the London government
in exile, and from 1942 he operated as general officer commanding
under the direct orders of the government. However, because of his
strong anti-Croatian and anti-communist attitudes, he found himself progressively isolated.

The left-wing partisan groups, on the other hand, had growing
support. The future was to lie with their superior military organization and popular social-revolutionary propaganda. From the
beginning, communist elements had successfully co-operated in the
formation of this movement and before long they took over its
organization. The rise of the man who had been general secretary
of the communist party of Yugoslavia since 1938, the Croatian-
born Josip Broz who was called 'Tito' and had the party name of
'Walter', to the leadership of the Yugoslav resistance movement
began in September 1941. Efforts to reach an understanding with
general Mihajlović had failed. It was thus that was initiated the
sharp animosity between the two partisan movements, which
now operated separately and against one another. Tito's unques-
tionable success finally persuaded the allies to withdraw their

support for Mihajlović and entrust the communist-controlled 'people's liberation army' with sole responsibility for the direction of the war in Yugoslavia.

Tito knew how to enlarge the basis of his movement. He mobilized the left-wing anti-fascist, patriotic forces on the proven lines of the people's front through the formation of the 'anti-fascist council for the national liberation of Yugoslavia' at Bihać in November 1942, so that he became the sole candidate for the political leadership of a liberated Yugoslavia when the occupation troops withdrew. The creation of a kind of provisional government within the framework of the 'anti-fascist council' by the founding of the 'national committee for the liberation of Yugoslavia' in November 1943, and the immediate forming of national-liberation committees in the areas freed by the army, prepared the ground for the new political order, and established the direction that the 'people's democracy' was to take. The same pattern was followed in the other Balkan countries where 'national fronts' against fascism and foreign domination sprang up after the liberation. They were a prelude to the general movement to the left and to political and social revolution on a grand scale.

This growth of revolution in the south-east European countries eased the way for close co-operation between the leftist partisan movement and Soviet foreign policy. The main cause, however, of the penetration of the Red Army deep into the centre of the Balkan peninsula during the final phase of the break-up of Hitler's Germany seems to have lain in the military planning of the western powers. Among them, south-eastern Europe had long been considered of secondary strategic importance. The British, who were primarily concerned with Greece and with their positions in the Mediterranean, ignored the Balkan hinterland. It was the entry of Soviet troops into Romania in April 1944–king Michael dismissing marshal Antonescu's government and officially announcing Romania's withdrawal from the war on August 23rd–and into Bulgaria on September 8th that belatedly caused Winston Churchill to raise the question of a bilateral agreement with Stalin over the demarcation of spheres of influence in the Balkans. During conversations in Moscow on October 9th, he managed to win

Stalin's consent to an arrangement by which ninety per cent of the control over the new Romania was to go to the Soviet Union and the same proportion to Great Britain for Greece. Seventy-five per cent of the control over Bulgaria was to go to the Soviet Union, but their control over Hungary and Yugoslavia was to be limited to fifty per cent. In the circumstances, it was a desperate effort on Churchill's part to negotiate at least a modest legal basis for the protection of the interests of the western powers in the Balkan states occupied by the Red Army. But events overtook this game with percentages.

The German withdrawal from Greece on September 2nd, 1944, left a deeply divided country. It took several years of bloody civil war between 1946 and 1949 to bring about the dissolution of the left-wing partisan organizations and their replacement with regular troops—a prerequisite for the transfer of political power to Papandreou's government, which had returned from exile. After king Michael's coup in August 1944, which had opened the way for the Red Army across the Danube, Bulgaria had tried to save herself from the threat of Soviet invasion by a reconstitution of her government and unilateral withdrawal from the war. But on September 5th the Soviet Union declared war on her and within a few days occupied the whole country without taking any notice of the offer of an armistice made by Kosta Muraviev, the prime minister. By the armistice terms of October 28th, which were dictated by Moscow, Bulgaria undertook to withdraw all her military units from Greece as well as from Yugoslavia and take an active part in the destruction of the remaining German forces. The authority of the government was transferred on September 9th to a transitional cabinet of the 'national front'. The nominal head of the government was colonel Kimon Georgiev, a leading member of the Zveno officers' organization, who had previously formed a government after the military coup in 1934. However, through their control of the ministries of the interior and justice, the communists had a firm grip on the mainsprings of power.

In Romania, the communists achieved their entry into the cabinet and paved their way to supremacy by the well-known tactic of the 'people's front'. As early as June 1944, an agreement between the communists and the leaders of the democratic parties, Maniu, Dinu Bratianu and Titel Petrescu, to form a people's front had set the stage, but this situation had lasted but a few months. For both the national peasants' party of Maniu and the national liberals of Bratianu had refused to join the national democratic front (the F.N.W.) of Dr. P. Groza. The progression towards a 'people's democracy' could no longer be halted, and on December 30th, 1947, king Michael abdicated.

During the last phase of the war in Yugoslavia, Tito's partisans fought their way out of Bosnia into Serbia and together with the Red Army occupied the capital, Belgrade, on October 20th, 1944. The prelude to this had been a conversation, unknown to the English, between Stalin and Tito on the island of Vis in September when future plans of action had been agreed. Although a coalition government was formed leading to the entry into the cabinet of Šubašić as minister of foreign affairs and of other members of the king's government in exile, only the communist-orientated people's front of Yugoslavia was admitted to the all-important elections of November 11th, 1945, that were to decide the country's future form of government. In protest against these restrictions, the middle-class politicians all resigned. On November 29th, 1945, the assembly responsible for determining the constitution proclaimed the 'Federal People's Republic of Yugoslavia'.

Albania followed the same path. From 1942 onwards, the time of the Italian occupation, a national resistance movement had developed around the left-wing 'national liberation movement' (the L.N.C. or Lëvizja Nacional Çlirimtare), which had been in close touch with Tito's partisans. The more conservative patriotic 'national front' (the B.K. or Balli Kombëtar), on the other hand, which had its supporters among the republican-minded land-owners of south Albania, had no comparable following. As in Yugoslavia no lasting understanding between the rival partisan groups was to be achieved, and from October 1943 there existed a state of open warfare between them. The withdrawal of Italy from the war in September 1943 precipitated a severe trial of strength with the German occupation forces. Again as in Yugoslavia, the outcome was favourable. The L.N.C. was to grow into the focal political force under communist influence, establishing itself as the new government of the country after the German retreat and preventing the restoration of the monarchy.

In the struggle for the leadership of the communist party, Enver Hoxha, who had been educated in the west, outmanoeuvred the radical wing led by Koci Xoxe that relied on the agricultural proletariat in the south, and drove into secession those elements in the L.N.C. who had any loyalty towards ex-king Zog and his former régime, such as Abas Kupi. Hoxha was so able to form a communist government in Tirana in November 1944. In a cleverly managed election on December 2nd, 1945, his 'democratic people's front' was given a mandate to introduce a republican constitution, and on January 11th, 1946, a republic was proclaimed.

All the Balkan states except Greece were to become communist, despite the fact that the allies had decided at Yalta that all liberated peoples should have the right to national self-determination, and that the communist parties had a relatively small number of adherents in the countries concerned. It was only in Yugoslavia and Bulgaria that the communists had had any significant early electoral successes going back as far as the 1920s. In the elections for the Belgrade Skupština in November 1920, they had won 58 out of 419 seats; in those of March 20th, 1920, for the Bulgarian assembly, the Sobranie, they had been returned as the second strongest party after the agrarian party led by Stambulijski. The opening up of a new reservoir of electoral support among the impoverished agricultural population, who were ready to accept the social revolutionary slogans, might have made up for the absence of a class-conscious industrial proletariat. But this is not what happened. The outcome was the result of the many obstacles to the work of the party and vigorous intervention on the part of the government to stop the development of any effective party organization. The votes gained by the communist party in Yugoslavia in 1920 had come from the agricultural areas of Macedonia and Montenegro, and not from the industrially advanced region of Slovenia. The party was banned in Yugoslavia shortly after its spectacular electoral success, and it remained illegal until the second world war. In Bulgaria, the communists lost their seats in parliament after the fall of Stambulijski in 1924. Their terrorist attempts in the 1920s, the climax of which was the devastating bomb explosion in the cathedral of Santa Sophia on April 16th, 1925, dissipated any outside sympathy they had.

There is no doubt that the official Comintern policy towards the nationality problem, that is, the problem of the right of minorities to self-determination, made it difficult for the communists in Yugoslavia to agitate there, as support for them would have been equivalent to support for separatist aims and would have given encouragement to nationalist factions to break away. It was Tito's unconditional backing of the principle of nationalism as a tactical weapon in the collective struggle for liberation that enabled the communists to make headway among the different groups. Judged against the background of later events, these underground communist activities in the Balkans were a decisive factor in the resistance movements. The illegal party organizations gained control of a sufficient number of military units to enable them to take over important tasks of leadership. Their rigid internal structure and uncompromising acceptance of the leadership principle were to prove that the communist partisan units had complete superiority over the other movements.

With the communist victory of the post-war period, a new era began in the history of south-eastern Europe. After being freed from the domination of Turks and Habsburgs, the Balkan countries had enjoyed a short, eventful period of transition and had then been forced into the framework of a new imperial system whose frontiers had been extended far into central Europe. The result was an economic and social revolution on a huge scale which through collectivization, the forced creation of heavy industry and total rejection of the 'bourgeois west' broke with centuries-old habits and brought into being, perhaps somewhat precipitately, the pattern of an industrial society based on the worker.

But the diversity of the Balkans was not lost in this process of massive intervention. The historical roots of the area were not forgotten, and they even helped enrich international Marxist dogmas by giving them national expression. The restoration of the territorial status quo in the peace treaties with Italy, Romania, Hungary, Bulgaria and Finland which were signed in Paris on February 10th, 1947, after tough negotiations, satisfied the demands of the victorious Balkan states. Hungary, Romania and Bulgaria had to give up the territories they had won in the period between the two wars; the 'second Vienna arbitration' of August 30th, 1940, was annulled and the arrangements that had been made for the parcelling out of Yugoslav territory were abrogated. The settlement of the Italian-Yugoslav frontier unleashed another wave of national emotion. In addition to Zadar and the island of Palagruža Yugoslavia finally gained the greater part of the province of Venezia Giulia including the port of Pula, the Isonzo valley and Istria, though she had to cede Trieste, which was declared a free state and placed under international control. The struggle for Trieste, which had lasted many years, did not come to an end until by the treaty of October 5th, 1954, Italy was given the civil administration of Zone A–that is, the city and its immediate surroundings–and Yugoslavia the administration of Zone B, the hinterland.

Full vent was also given to national feelings in a bloody settlement of accounts with the Croatian Ustaša highlighted by the tragedy of Bleiburg of May 1945 when the units that had capitulated were handed over to Tito. The expulsion of Yugoslavs of German ethnic origin was carried out with similar forcefulness. The former substantial German section of the Yugoslav population amounting to some half a million people has virtually disappeared today. But Tito's adherence to the federal principle as his solution to the nationalities problem, which had paralysed the internal development of Yugoslavia between the two wars, was more auspicious. Following the Soviet constitution of 1936, the Yugoslav constitution of January 31st, 1946, established a federation consisting of six people's republics, Serbia, Croatia, Slovenia, Bosnia-Herzegovina, Montenegro and Macedonia, together with an autonomous territory largely populated by Albanians–Kosovo-Metohija.

Tito was to take the federal idea still further and extend it to relations between the other Balkan people's democracies: it was in fact a resumption of the idea of a Balkan federation in a communist context. This began to assume a concrete shape in the negotiations with the Bulgarian prime minister Dimitrov leading to the protocol of Bled of August 1st, 1946, but opposition from Moscow put an end to the matter. During the war years, Stalin had found Tito an awkward, independent-minded ally, and the possibility of a strong Balkan alliance under Yugoslav leadership was bound to make Stalin feel nervous with regard to his position of authority over the network of Soviet satellites. In the sensational conflict within the Cominform in June 1948 he forced Tito to break with international communism, and so drove him into isolation. As a counter-move, Tito sought a rapprochement with the non-communist countries of south-eastern Europe, making a 'Balkan pact' with Greece and Turkey on August 9th, 1954, which included guarantees of territorial integrity and a commitment to give military assistance against any aggressor. It was not until after Stalin's death in 1953 when the direction of Soviet foreign policy was changed that a new period in diplomatic relations between the Balkan states began.

Since then, fresh life has been injected into the Balkan people's democracies as various alternatives have offered themselves. Albania had already taken the opportunity to free herself from the dominating influence of her Yugoslav neighbour in 1948, which was exercised through an important minority amounting to a third of the Albanian population, and sought direct support from the government in Moscow; and after Bulganin and Khrushchev's visit to Belgrade of May 26th to June 2nd, 1956, offering atonement for past misdeeds and publicly announcing the policy of de-stalinization, she adapted herself to the new situation by becoming pro-Chinese.

At the present moment there are signs of increasing self-confidence among the Balkan states, who have been making definite attempts to achieve greater independence and cast off the political and economic domination of their Soviet ally. Hard-pressed by unavoidable development problems their governments have been trying new and sometimes distinctive lines of action which have tended more and more to find their justification in national history. Even communism as the general ideology of the region, creating unity out of Balkan diversity, will in the long run prove unable to escape the influence of an idealized past.

BIBLIOGRAPHY

The following bibliography is mainly limited to works written in western European languages. The only works written in the original Balkan languages that are included are the comprehensive surveys that are accepted as valid today.

I

BIBLIOGRAPHY AND GENERAL SOURCES

BOROV, T., DEMBOWSKA, M., TOMESCU, M., DRTINA, J., KUZMÍK, J., and BÉLLEY, P., *Die Bibliographie in den europäischen Ländern der Volksdemokratie. Entwicklung und gegenwärtiger Stand* (Bibliography of the peoples' democracies in Europe. Development and present situation), Leipzig, 1960.

TEICH, G., 'Bibliographie der Bibliographien Südosteuropas. Ein Beitrag zur Bibliographie über den Gessamtraum Südosteuropa sowie über Albanien, Griechenland und die Türkei'. (Bibliography of bibliographies of south-east Europe. A contribution to the bibliography of the entire region of southeastern Europe including Albania, Greece and Turkey), *Wirtschaftswissenschaftliche Südosteuropa-Forschung. Grundlagen und Erkenntnisse* (Economic studies of southeastern Europe. Principles and knowledge), Munich, 1963, pp. 177–213 (*Südosteuropa-Schriften*, Southeast Europe, vol. 4).

HORECKY, PAUL L. (ed.), *Southeastern Europe. A Guide to Basic Publications*, Chicago, London, 1969.

The Balkans. A Selected List of References, vols. 1–5, Washington, 1945, (United States Library of Congress, Division of Bibliography).

STRAKHOVSKY, L. I. (ed), *A Handbook of Slavic Studies*, Cambridge, Mass., 1949.

DIELS, P., *Die slavischen Völker: Mit einer Literaturübersicht von Alexander Adamczyk* (The Slav peoples. Including a survey of Literature by Alexander Adamczyk) Wiesbaden, 1963 (publications of the East European Institute, Munich, vol. 11).

KASTRATI, J., *Bibliografi Shqipe* (29 Nov. 1944 to 31 Nov. 1958), Tirana, 1959.

PUNDEFF, M. V., *Bulgaria. A Bibliographic Guide*, Washington, 1965.

TADIĆ, J. (ed.), *Dix Années d'historiographie yougoslave 1945–1955* (Ten years of Yugoslav historical writings 1945–1955), Belgrade, 1955.

GRAFENAUER, B., ŠIDAK, J., TADIĆ, J., (eds.), *Historiographie yougoslave 1955–1965* (Yugoslav historical publications 1955–1965), Belgrade, 1965.

HILLGRUBER, A., *Südosteuropa im Zweiten Weltkrieg. Literaturbericht und Bibliographie* (South-eastern Europe in the second world war. Bibliography and review of literature), Frankfurt am Main, 1962, (Library of Contemporary History publications. World war books, vol. 1).

Current Bibliography:

Südosteuropa-Bibliographie (South-eastern Europe bibliography):
  vol. 1, 1945–1950, 2 parts, Munich, 1956–1959.
  vol. 2, 1951–1955, edited by Gertrud Krallert-Sattler in 2 parts, Munich, 1960–1962.
  vol. 3, 1956–1960, part 1, Munich, 1964; part 2, Munich, 1968.
  vol. 4, 1961–1965, part 1, Munich, 1971.

II

NATIONAL HISTORY AND FOLK-LORE, LANGUAGE AND POPULATION

CVIJIĆ, J., *La Péninsule balkanique. Géographie humaine* (The Balkan peninsula. Human geography), Paris, 1918.

BLANC, A., *Géographie des Balkans* (Geography of the Balkans), Paris, 1965, ('*Que Sais-je?*', no. 1154).

MAULL, O., 'Einheit und Gliederung Südosteuropas' (The unity and structure of south-east Europe), *Leipziger Vierteljahresschrift für Südosteuropa*, 1, 4 (1937), pp. 3–20.

GAVAZZI, M., 'Die Kulturgeographische Gliederung Südosteuropas (Ein Entwurf)' (Cultural influences in south-eastern Europe. An outline), *Südost-Forschungen*, 15, 1956, pp. 5–21.

ANCEL, J., *Peuples et nations des Balkans. Géographie politique* (Peoples and nations of the Balkans. Political geography), 2nd ed., Paris, 1941.

MATL, J., 'Die Kultur der Südslawen' (The culture of the southern Slavs), *Handbuch der Kulturgeschichte*, 101–105, nos. 1–5, Frankfurt am Main, 1966.

SCHNEEWEIS, E., *Grundriss des Volksglaubens and Volksbrauchs der Serbokroaten* (Outline of religious beliefs and customs of the Serbo-Croats), Celje, 1935.

GESEMANN, G., *Heroische Lebensform. Zur Literatur und Wesenskunde der balkanischen Patriarchalität* (A heroic way of life. Literature and ontology of the Balkan patriarchy), Berlin, 1943.

SANDERS, I., *Balkan Village*, Lexington, 1949.

HALPERN, J. M., *A Serbian Village*, New York, 1958.

Südosteuropa-Schriften (Southeast-European writing), especially:
   vol. 1, *Völker und Kulturen Südosteuropas. Kulturhistorische Beiträge* (Peoples and cultures of south-eastern Europe. Contributions to cultural history), Munich, 1959.
   vol. 6, *Die Kultur Südosteuropas. Ihre Geschichte und ihre Ausdrucksformen* (The culture of south-eastern Europe. Its history and forms of expression), Munich, 1964.
   vol. 7, *Volksmusik Südosteuropas* (Folk music in south-eastern Europe.) Munich, 1966.

Die Volkskultur der südosteuropäischen Völker (The national culture of the south-east-European peoples), Munich, 1962, (*Südosteuropa-Jahrbuch*, vol. 6).

SANDFELD, K., *Linguistique balkanique. Problèmes et résultats* (Balkan language studies. Problems and findings), Paris, 1930.

POPOVIĆ, I., *Geschichte der serbokroatischen Sprache*. (History of the Serbo-Croat language), Wiesbaden, 1960 (*Bibliotheca Slavica*).

PUŞCARIU, S., *Die rumänische Sprache. Ihr Wesen und ihre volkliche Prägung* (The Romanian language. Its nature and popular expression), Leipzig, 1943.

LEMERLE, P., 'Invasions et migrations dans les Balkans depuis la fin de l'époque romaine jusqu'au VIIIe siècle' ('Invasions and migrations in the Balkans from the end of the Roman period to the eighth century'), *Revue historique*, 211, (1954), pp. 265–308.

RIEDL, F. H., *Das Südostdeutschtum in den Jahren 1918–1945* (South-eastern Germans in the years 1918–1945), Munich, 1962, (*Südostdeutsches Kulturwerk, Kleine Südostreihe*, vol. 3).

LADAS, S. P., *The Exchange of Minorities: Bulgaria, Greece, Turkey*, New York, 1932.

MACARTNEY, C. A., *National States and National Minorities*, London, 1934.

FRUMKIN, G., *Population Changes in Europe since 1939. A Study of Population Changes in Europe during and since World War II as Shown by the Balance Sheets of Twenty-four European Countries*, New York, 1951.

Bevölkerungsentwicklungen in Südosteuropa. Jugoslawien, Ungarn, Rumänien (Population development in south-eastern Europe. Yugoslavia, Hungary, Romania), Munich, 1964 (*Untersuchungen zur Gegenwartskunde Südosteuropas*, Südost-Institut, Munich, vol. 5).

III

COMPREHENSIVE SURVEYS

1. General, Ancient Times, Middle Ages

MILLER, W., *The Balkans, Roumania, Bulgaria, Servia and Montenegro* (with a new chapter containing their history from 1896 to 1922), 3rd ed., London, 1923.

FORBES, N., TOYNBEE, A. J., MITRANY, D., HOGARTH, G., *The Balkans. A History of Bulgaria, Serbia, Greece, Rumania, Turkey*, Oxford, 1915.

SCHEVILL, F., *History of the Balkan Peninsula. From the Earliest Times to the Present Day*, New York, 1922, reprinted New York, 1966.

STADTMÜLLER, G., *Geschichte Südosteuropas* (History of south-eastern Europe) Munich, 1950.

RANDA, A., *Der Balkan. Schülsselraum der Weltgeschichte. Von Thrake zu Byzanz* (The Balkans. Key area in world history. From Thrace to Byzantium), Graz, Salzburg, Vienna, 1949.

RANDA, A., *Der Balkan von Diokletian bis Tito* (The Balkans from Diocletian to Tito), Zurich, 1950.

RISTELHUEBER, R., *Histoire des peuples balkaniques* (History of the Balkan peoples), Paris, 1950.

DVORNIK, F., *The Slavs, their Early History and Civilisation*, Boston, 1956.

HALECKI, O., *Grenzraum des Abendlandes. Eine Geschichte Ostmitteleuropas* (Frontier area of western civilisation. A history of the eastern part of central Europe), Salzburg, 1956.

FARKAS, J. VON, *Südosteuropa. Ein Überblick* (South-eastern Europe. A review), Göttingen, 1955.

JELAVICH, CH. and B., *The Balkans*, Englewood Cliffs, New Jersey, 1965.

BRAUN, M., *Die Slawen auf dem Balkan bis zur Befreiung von der türkischen Herrschaft* (The Slavs in the Balkans up to the liberation from Turkish rule), Leipzig, 1941.

HUSSEY, J. M. (ed.), *Byzantium and its Neighbours*, Cambridge, 1966 (*Cambridge Medieval History*, vol. 4, part 1).

STAVRIANOS, L. S., *The Balkans since 1453*, New York, 1958.

BERNATH, M., 'Die Südslawen' (The southern Slavs), *Die Welt der Slawen* (The world of the Slavs), ed. Hans Kohn, vol. 1; *Die West und Südslawen* (The western and southern Slavs), Frankfurt, Hamburg, 1960, pp. 209-87.

MATL, J., *Südslawische Studien* (Southern Slav studies), Munich, 1965, (*Südosteuropäische Arbeiten*, no. 63).

VALJAVEC, F., *Ausgewählte Aufsätze* (Selected essays), Munich, 1963 (*Südosteuropäische Arbeiten*, no. 60).

2. Modern Times

JELAVICH, DH. and B. (eds.), *The Balkans in Transition. Essays on the Development of Balkan Life and Politics since the Eighteenth Century*, Berkeley and Los Angeles, 1963.

ANCEL, J., *Manuel historique de la question d'Orient (1792-1930)* (Historical manual on the eastern question), 4th ed., Paris, 1931.

HEYMANN, E., *Balkan, Kriege, Bündnisse, Revolutionen. 150 Jahre Politik und Schicksal* (The Balkans. Wars, treaties, revolutions. 150 years of politics and destiny), Berlin, 1938.

STAVRIANOS, L. S., *The Balkans 1815-1914*, New York, 1963.

ARNAKIS, GEORGE G., *The Near East in Modern Times*, vol. 1: *The Ottoman Empire and the Balkan States to 1900*, Austin and New York, 1969.

GEWEHR, W. M., *The Rise of Nationalism in the Balkans 1800-1930*, New York, 1931.

MOSCHOPOULOS, N., *La Presse dans la renaissance balkanique* (The press in the period of Balkan recovery), Athens, 1931.

STAVRIANOS, L. S., *Balkan Federation. A History of the Movement Toward Balkan Unity in Modern Times*, Northampton, Mass., 1944, new ed. Hamden, Conn., 1964.

KANN, R. A., *Das Nationalitätenproblem der Habsburgermonarchie. Geschichte und Ideengehalt der nationalen Bestrebungen vom Vormärz bis zur Auflösung des Reiches im Jahre 1918* (The problem of nationalities in the Habsburg monarchy. History of nationalist movements from 1848 to the break-up of the Empire in 1918), vols. 1-2, Graz, Cologne, 1964.

DJORDJEVIĆ, D., *Revolutions nationales des peuples balkaniques 1804-1914* (National revolutions of the Balkan peoples 1804-1914), Belgrade, 1965.

JELAVICH, CH., *Tsarist Russia and Balkan Nationalism. Russian Influence in the Internal Affairs of Bulgaria and Serbia, 1879-1886*, Berkeley and Los Angeles, 1958.

WOLFF, R. L., *The Balkans in Our Time*, Cambridge, Mass., 1956.

SETON-WATSON, H., *Eastern Europe between the Wars 1918–1941*, Cambridge, 1946.

MITRANY, D., *The Effect of the War in Southeastern Europe. Economic and Social History of the World War*, New Haven, 1946.

MACARTNEY, C. A., and PALMER, A. W., *Independent Eastern Europe. A History*, London, New York, 1962, paperback ed. 1966.

South-eastern Europe. A political and economic survey, London, 1939.

KISZLING, R., *Die militärischen Vereinbarungen der Kleinen Entente, 1929–1937* (Military agreements of the Little Entente, 1929–1937), Munich, 1959, (*Südosteuropäische Arbeiten*, no. 54).

KERNER, R. J., and HOWARD, H. N., *The Balkan Conferences and the Balkan Entente 1930–1933. A Study in the Recent History of the Balkan and Near Eastern Peoples*, Berkeley, 1936.

TOYNBEE, A. and V. M. (eds.), *Survey of International Affairs 1939–1946: Hitler's Europe*, London, 1954.

3. Post-war Developments, the Present

BETTS, R. R. (ed.), *Central and South East Europe 1945–1948*, London, New York, 1950.

SETON-WATSON, H., *The East European Revolution*, London, 1950.

FETJÖ, F., *Histoire des Démocraties populaires* (History of the popular democracies), Paris, 1952.

BIRKE, E. and NEUMANN, R. (eds.), *Die Sowjetisierung Ost-Mitteleuropas. Untersuchungen zu ihrem Ablauf in den einzelnen Ländern* (The Sovietization of eastern Europe. Investigation into its progress in the individual countries), vol. 1, Frankfurt, Berlin, 1959.

MITRANY, D., *Marx against the Peasant. A Study in Social Dogmatism*, London, 1951.

East-Central Europe under the Communists (Mid-European Center):

SKENDI, ST. (ed.), *Albania*, New York, 1956.

DELLIN, L. A. D. (ed.), *Bulgaria*, New York, 1957.

FISCHER-GALATI, ST. (ed.), *Romania*, New York, 1957.

BYRNES, R. F. (ed.), *Yugoslavia*, New York, 1958.

Wissenschaftlicher Dienst Südosteuropa. Quellen und Berichte über Staat, Verwaltung, Bevölkerung, Wirtschaft, Wissenschaft und Veröffentlichungen in Südosteuropa (Publications on south-eastern Europe. Sources and reports on government, administration, population, trade, research, and publications in south-eastern Europe), Munich 1, 1952: contemporary reporting.

IV

INDIVIDUAL BALKAN COUNTRIES

1. Albania

Historia e Shqipërisë në tre vëllime (A history of Albania in three volumes), vols. 1 and 2, Tirana, 1959–1965.

FRASHERI, K., *The History of Albania. A Brief Survey*, Tirana, 1964.

ARŠ, G. L., SENKEVIČ, I. G., and SMIRNOVA, N. D., *Kratkaja istorija Albanii* (A short history of Albania), Moscow, 1965.

STADMÜLLER, G., *Forschungen zur albanischen Frühgeschichte* (Research on the early history of Albania), 2nd ed., Wiesbaden, 1966 (*Albanische Forschungen, 2*).

SKENDI, ST., *The Albanian National Awakening 1878–1912*, Princeton, N.J., 1967.

SWIRE, J., *Albania. The Rise of a Kingdom*, London, 1929.

AMERY, J., *Sons of the Eagle. A Study in Guerilla War*, London, 1948.

SKENDI, ST. (ed.), *Albania*, New York, 1956.

GRIFFITH, W. E., *Albania and the Sino-Soviet Rift*, Cambridge, Mass., 1963.

2. Bulgaria

JIREČEK, C., *Geschichte der Bulgaren* (History of the Bulgarians), Prague, 1876.

ZLATARSKI, V. N., *Istorija na bŭlgarskata dŭržava prěz srědnitě věkove* (History of the Bulgars in the Middle Ages), 3 vols. in 4, Sofia, 1918–1940.

SLATARSKI, W. N., and STANEFF, N., *Geschichte der Bulgaren* (History of the Bulgarian people), vols. 1–2, Leipzig, 1917.

Istorija na Bŭlgarija (History of Bulgaria), ed. D. Kosev and others, 2nd ed., vols. 1–3, Sofia, 1961–1964.

KOSSEV, D., CHRISTOV, CH., and ANGELOV, D., *Bulgarische Geschichte* (Bulgarian history), Sofia, 1963.

EVANS, ST. G., *A Short History of Bulgaria*, London, 1960.

RUNCIMAN, S., *A History of the First Bulgarian Empire*, London, 1930.

WOLFF, R. L., 'The second Bulgarian Empire. Its origin and history to 1204', *Speculum*, 24 (1949), pp. 167–206.

MACDERMOTT, M., *A History of Bulgaria 1393–1885*, London, 1962.

HAJEK, A., *Bulgarien unter der Türkenherrschaft* (Bulgaria under Turkish rule), Stuttgart, 1925.

HAJEK, A., *Bulgariens Befreiung und staatliche Entwicklung unter seinem ersten Fürsten* (Liberation of Bulgaria and political development under its first prince), Munich, Berlin, 1939.

BLACK, C. E., *The Establishment of Constitutional Government in Bulgaria*, Princeton, 1943.

DELLIN, L. A. D. (ed.), *Bulgaria*, New York, 1957.

ROTHSCHILD, J., *The Communist Party of Bulgaria. Origins and Development 1883–1936*, New York, 1959.

SAKÂZOV, I., *Bulgarische Wirtschaftgeschichte* (Economic history of Bulgaria), Berlin, Leipzig, 1929.

3. Yugoslavia and its Regions

KOSTELSKI, Z., *The Yugoslavs. The History of the Yugoslavs and their States to the Creation of Yugoslavia*, New York, 1952.

Istorija naroda Jugoslavije (History of the people of Yugoslavia), vols. 1–2, Belgrade, 1953–1960 (with a parallel edition in Slovene and Croatian): it covers the period up to the end of the eighteenth century).

Pregled istorije jugoslovenskih naroda (Short history of the Yugoslav people), vol. 1, Belgrade, 1963.

AUTY, P., *Yugoslavia*, London, 1965

CLISSOLD, ST. (ed.), *A Short History of Yugoslavia. From Early Times to 1966*, Cambridge, 1966.

GESEMANN, G., HEYMANN, E., MÄRZ, J., OERTZEN, F. W. VON, SCHMAUS, A., STELÈ, F., and WIRSING, G., *Das Königreich Südslawien* (The kingdom of the southern Slavs), Leipzig, 1935.

Yugoslavia, London, 1961; vol. 1, HEPPELL, M., *The History of the Yugoslav Lands up to the Outbreak of the First World War*; vol. 2, SINGLETON, F. B., *The Birth of Yugoslavia and the Modern State*.

HAUMONT, É., *La Formation de la Yougoslavie (XVe–XXe siècles)* (The creation of Yugoslavia), Paris, 1930.

LUDAT, H. (ed.), *Jugoslawien zwischen West und Ost. Probleme seiner Geschichte, Wirtschaft und Politik* (Yugoslavia between east and west. Problems of the country's history, economics and politics), Giessen, 1961.

MARKERT, W. (ed.), *Jugoslawien* (Yugoslavia), Cologne, Graz, 1954 (*Osteuropa-Handbuch*, vol. 1).

KERNER, R. J. (ed.), *Yugoslavia*, Berkeley, 1949.

BYRNES, R. F. (ed.), *Yugoslavia*, New York, 1957.

HOPTNER, J. B., *Yugoslavia in Crisis 1934–1941*, New York, London, 1962.

TOMASEVICH, J., *Peasants, Politics and Economic Change in Yugoslavia*, London, Stanford, Calif., 1955.

LAZITCH, B., *Tito et la révolution yougoslave, 1937–1956* (Tito and the Yugoslav revolution, 1937–1956), Paris, 1957.

ULAM, A. B., *Titoism and the Cominform*, Cambridge, 1952.

AUTY, P., *Tito, a Biography*, London, 1970.

DUROSELLE, J.-B., *Le Conflit de Trieste, 1943–1954* (The conflict of Trieste, 1943–1954), Brussels, 1966.

BASS, R., and MARBURY, E. (eds.), *The Soviet-Yugoslav Controversy, 1948–58. A Documentary Record*, New York, 1959.

GASTEYGER, K. (ed.), *Die feindlichen Brüder. Jugoslawiens neuer Konflikt mit dem Ostblock 1958. Ein Dokumentenband* (The hostile brothers. Yugoslavia's new conflict with the eastern block, 1958. A documentation), Bern, 1960.

(a) Serbia

KANITZ, F. PH., *Das Königreich Serbien und das Serbenvolk von der Römerzeit bis zur Gegenwart* (The Serbian kingdom and its peoples from Roman times to the present day), vols. 1–3, Leipzig, 1904–1914.

JIREČEK, C., *Geschichte der Serben* (History of the Serbs), vols. 1–2, 1, Gotha 1911–1918.

JIREČEK, C., *Staat und Gesellschaft im mittelalterlichen Serbien. Studien zur Kulturgeschichte des 13.–15. Jahrhunderts* (State and society in Serbia in the Middle Ages. Studies of the history of culture in the thirteenth and fifteenth centuries), vols. 1–4, Vienna, 1912–1919 (*Denkschriften der Kaiserlichen Akademie der Wissenschaften in Wien, Phil.-hist. Klasse*).

MLADENOVITCH, M., *L'État serbe au moyen âge. Son caractère* (The Serbian state in the Middle Ages. Its character), Paris, 1931.

NOVAKOVIĆ, ST., *Die Wiedergeburt des serbischen Staates (1804–1813)* (The rebirth of the Serbian states), Sarajevo, 1912.

VUCINICH, W. S., *Serbia between East and West. The Events of 1903–1908*, Stanford, Calif., 1954.

MCCLELLAN, W. D., *Svetozar Marković and the Origins of Balkan Socialism*, Princeton, N.J., 1964.

(b) *Montenegro*

Istorija Crne Gore (History of Montenegro), vol. 1, Cetinje, 1967.

(c) *Croatia*

ŠIŠIĆ, F. VON, *Geschichte der Kroaten* (History of the Croats), part 1, (to 1102), Zagreb, 1917.

KISZLING, R., *Die Kroaten. Der Schicksalsweg eines Südslawenvolkes* (The Croatians. The destiny of a southern Slav people), Graz, Cologne, 1956.

PREVEDEN, F., *A History of the Croatian People from their Arrival on the Shores of the Adriatic to the Present Day*, New York, 1955.

GULDESCU, ST., *History of Medieval Croatia*, The Hague, 1964.

HORY, L., and BROSZAT, M., *Der kroatische Ustascha-Staat 1941–1945* (The Croatian Ustaša state 1941–1945), Stuttgart, 1964 (*Schriftenreihe der Vierteljahrshefte für Zeitgeschichte*.

(d) *Bosnia*

KLAIĆ, V., *Geschichte Bosniens von den ältesten Zeiten bis zum Verfalle des Königreiches* (History of Bosnia from earliest times to the break-up of the Empire), Leipzig, 1885.

ĆIRKOVIĆ, S., *Istorija srednjovekovne bosanske države* (History of the Bosnian state in the Middle Ages), Belgrade, 1964.

SUGAR, P. F., *Industrialization of Bosnia-Hercegovina 1878–1918*, Seattle, 1964.

(e) *Slovenia*

MAL, J., *Probleme aus der Frühgeschichte der Slowenen* (Early history of the Slovene people and their problems), Ljubljana, 1939.

GRAFENAUER, B., *Zgodovina slovenskega naroda* (History of the Slovene people), vols. 1-5, Ljubljana, 1954-1962.

LONĆAR, D., *The Slovenes. A Social History*, Cleveland, 1939.

(f) *Dalmatia*

VOJNOVITCH, L. DE, *Histoire de Dalmatie* (History of Dalmatia), vols. 1-2, Paris, 1934.

JIREČEK, C., *Die Romanen in den Städten Dalmatiens während des Mittelalters* (The Latin peoples in the Dalmatian cities during the Middle Ages), vols. 1-3, Vienna, 1901-1904 (*Denkschriften der Kaiserlichen Akademie der Wissenschaften in Wien, Phil.-hist. Klasse*).

(g) *Macedonia*

BRAILSFORD, H. N., *Macedonia. Its Races and Their Future*, London, 1906.

BARKER, E., *Macedonia. Its Place in Balkan Power Politics*, London, 1950.

WILKINSON, H. R., *Maps and Politics. A Review of the Ethnographic Cartography of Macedonia*, Liverpool, 1951.

4. Romania

PHILIPPIDE, A., *Originea Românilor* (The Romanians and their origins), vols. 1-2, Jassy, 1923-1927.

SETON-WATSON, R. W., *A History of the Romanians from Roman Times to the Completion of Unity*, Cambridge, 1934, new ed. 1963.

JORGA, N., *Histoire des Roumains et de la Romanité orientale* (History of the Romanian people and Roman culture in eastern Europe), vols. 1-10, Bucharest, 1937-1945.

JORGA, N., *Byzance après Byzance. Continuation de 'l'Histoire de la vie byzantine'* (Byzantium after Byzantium. Continuation of 'The history of the Byzantine way of life'), Bucharest, 1935.

GIURESCU, C., *Istoria românilor* (History of the Romanian people), vols. 1-3, Bucharest, 1938-1946.

Istoria Romîniei (History of Romania), vols. 1-4, Bucharest 1960-1964: it goes up to 1878.

RIKER, T. W., *The Making of Roumania. A Study of an International Problem, 1856-1866*, London, Oxford, 1931.

SCHMIDT, E., *Die verfassungsrechtliche und politische Struktur des rumänischen Staates in ihrer historischen Entwicklung* (The constitution and political structure of the Romanian state and its historical development), Munich, 1932.

HAUFE, H., *Die Wandlung der Volksordnung im rumänischen Altreich. Agrarverfassung und Bevölkerungsentwicklung im 19. und 20 Jahrhundert* (The change of ethnic structure in the old kingdom of Romania. Agrarian constitution and population development in the nineteenth and twentieth centuries), Stuttgart, 1939.

MITRANY, D., *The Land and the Peasant in Rumania. The War and Agrarian Reform (1917–1921)*, London, 1930.

ROBERTS, H. L., *Rumania. Political Problems of an Agrarian State*, New Haven, London, 1951.

HÖPKER, W., *Rumänien diesseits und jenseits der Karpathen* (Romania on the near side and far side of the Carpathians), Munich, 1936.

HILLGRUBER, A., *Hitler, König Carol und Marschall Antonescu. Die deutschrumänischen Beziehungen 1938–1944* (Hitler, King Carol and Marshall Antonescu. German and Romanian relations 1938–1944), Wiesbaden, 1954.

FISCHER-GALATI, ST. (ed.), *Romania*, New York, 1957.

FISCHER-GALATI, ST., *The New Rumania. From People's Democracy to Socialist Republic*, Cambridge, Mass., London, 1967.

DAICOVICIU, C., and CONSTANTINESCU, M. (eds.), *Brève histoire de la Transylvanie* (Short history of Transylvania), Bucharest, 1965 (*Bibliotheca historica Romaniae*, monograph III).

V

BORDER AREAS, OUTSIDE INFLUENCES

CASSON, ST., *Macedonia, Thrace and Illyria. Their Relations to Greece from the Earliest Times Down to the Time of Philip, Son of Amyntas*, Oxford, 1929.

BENGTSON, H., *Griechische Geschichte von den Anfängen bis in die römanische Kaiserzeit* (Greek history from the beginning to the time of the Roman empire), Munich, 1950 (*Handbuch der Altertumswissenschaft*, vol. III, 4).

KORNEMANN, E., *Weltgeschichte des Mittelmeer-Raumes von Philipp II von Makedonien bis Muhammed* (A history of the Mediterranean area from Philip II of Macedonia to Mohammed), vols. 1–2, Munich, 1948–1949.

WERNER, R., 'Geschichte des Donau-Schwarzmeer-Raumes im Altertum' (History of the Danube-Black Sea area in ancient times), *Abriss der Geschichte antiker Randkulturen*, Munich, 1961, pp. 83–150 (*Oldenbourgs Abriss der*

Weltgeschichte, with references to the Illyrians, Galatians and Thracians, among others.)

WIESNER, J., *Die Thraker. Studien zu einem versunkenen Volk des Balkans* (The Thracians. Studies on a submerged race in the Balkans), Stuttgart, 1963 (*Urban-Bücherei*, no. 41).

OSTROGORSKY, G., *Geschichte des byzantinischen Staates* (History of the Byzantine empire), 3rd ed., Munich, 1963 (*Byzantinisches Handbuch im Rahmen des Handbuchs der Altertumswissenschaft*, part 1, vol. 2).

HUSSEY, J. M. (ed.), *The Byzantine Empire*, Cambridge, 1966–1967 (*Cambridge Modern History*, vol. 4, parts 1–2).

OBOLENSKY, D., *The Byzantine Commonwealth: Eastern Europe 500–1453*, London, 1971.

NICOL, D. M., *The Despotate of Epiros*, Oxford, 1957.

HOPF, C., *Geschichte Griechenlands vom Beginn des Mittelalters bis auf unsere Zeit* (History of Greece from the beginning of the Middle Ages to the present day), vols. 1–2, Leipzig, 1867–1868, new ed., New York, 1960 (Ersch-Gruber, *Allgemeine Encyklopädie der Wissenschaften und Künste*, vols. 85–86).

ZAKYTHINOS, D. A., Ἡ πολιτικὴ ἱστορία τῆς νεωτέρας Ἑλλάδος. Εἰσαγωγικὰ μαθήματα (Political history of modern Greece. An introduction), Athens, 1962.

VAKALOPOULOS, A., Ἱστορία τοῦ νέου Ἑλληνισμοῦ (History of modern Greece), vols. 1–3 so far published, Thessalonica, 1961–1968 (up to 1669).

DRIAULT, E., and LHÉRITIER, M., *Histoire diplomatique de la Grèce de 1821 à nos jours* (Diplomatic history of Greece from 1821 to the present day), vols. 1–5, Paris, 1925–1926.

SVORONOS, N. G., *Histoire de la Grèce moderne* (History of modern Greece), Paris, 1953 (*Que sais-je?* no. 578).

BROCKLEMANN, C., *Geschichte der islamischen Völker und Staaten* (History of the Islamic peoples and states), 2nd ed., Munich, Berlin, 1943.

WERNER, E., *Die Geburt einer Grossmacht. Die Osmanen (1300–1481). Ein Beitrag zur Genesis des türkischen Feudalismus* (The birth of a great power. The Ottoman empire (1300–1481). Work on the origins of Turkish feudalism), Berlin, 1966.

HAMMER-PURGSTALL, J. VON, *Geschichte des osmanischen Reiches* (History of the Ottoman empire), vols. 1–10, Budapest, 1827–1835, reprinted Graz, 1963.

ZINKEISEN, J. W., *Geschichte des osmanischen Reiches in Europa* (History of the Ottoman empire in Europe), vols. 1–7, Hamburg, Gotha, 1840–1863.

JORGA, N., *Geschichte des osmanischen Reiches nach den Quellen dargestellt* (History of the Ottoman empire based on sources), vols. 1–5, Gotha, 1908–1913.

KISSLING, H.-J., 'Das osmanische Reich bis 1774' (The Ottoman empire up to 1774), *Handbuch der Orientalistik*, section 1, vol. 6, section 3, Leiden, Cologne, 1959, pp. 3–46.

BABINGER, F., *Beiträge zur Frühgeschichte der Türkenherrschaft in Rumelien* (Material on the early history of Turkish rule in Rumelia, 14th–15th centuries), Brünn, Munich, Vienna, 1944.

BABINGER, F., *Aufsätze und Abhandlungen zur Geschichte Südosteuropas und der Levante* (Essays on the history of south-eastern Europe and the Levant), vols. 1–2, Munich, 1962–1966 (*Südosteuropa-Schriften*, vols. 3 and 8).

BABINGER, F., *Mehmed der Eroberer und seine Zeit. Weltenstürmer einer Zeitenwende* (Mohammed the conqueror and his times. World conqueror at a turning point in history), 2nd ed., Munich, 1959.

DUDA, H. W., *Balkantürkische Studien* (Studies on the Turks in the Balkans), Vienna, 1949.

GEGAJ, A., *L'Albanie et l'invasion turque au XVe siecle* (Albania and the Turkish invasion in the fifteenth century), Louvain, 1937.

VAUGHAN, D., *Europe and the Turk. A Pattern of Alliances 1350–1700*, Liverpool, 1954.

GIBB, H. A. R., and BOWEN, H., *Islamic Society and the West. A Study of the Impact of Western Civilization on Moslem Culture in the Near East*, 2 parts, London, 1950–1960.

SAX, C. VON, *Geschichte des Machtverfalls der Türkei bis Ende des 19. Jahrhunderts und die Phasen der 'orientalischen Frage' bis auf die Gegenwart, 2. bis zum Konstantinopler Frieden (29 September 1913)* (History of the break-up of Turkish rule to the end of the nineteenth century and the various phases of the 'eastern question' to the present day. (2nd ed.) To the Treaty of Constantinople (29th Sept. 1913)), revised ed., Vienna, 1913.

MILLER, W., *The Ottoman Empire and Its Successors 1801–1936*, Cambridge, 1934, New York, 1936.

HOWARD, H. N., *The Partition of Turkey. A Diplomatic History 1913–1923*, Norman, Oklahoma, 1931.

HÓMAN, B., *Geschichte des ungarischen Mittelalters* (History of Hungary in the Middle Ages), vols. 1–2, Berlin, 1940–1953.

FARKAS, J. VON, *Ungarns Geschichte und Kultur in Dokumenten* (Documents on the history and civilization of Hungary), Wiesbaden, 1955.

UHLIRZ, K.-M., *Handbuch der Geschichte Österreichs und seiner Nachbarländer Böhmen und Ungarn* (Handbook on the history of Austria and its neighbours Bohemia and Hungary), vols. 1–4, Graz, 1927–1944; 2nd ed., *Handbuch der Geschichte*

Österreich-Ungarns (Handbook on the history of Austria-Hungary), vol. 1 up to 1526, Graz, Vienna, Cologne, 1963.

ROTHENBERG, G. E., *The Austrian Military Border in Croatia 1522–1747*, Urbana, 1960.

ROTHENBURG, G. E., *The Military Border in Croatia 1740–1881. A Study of an Imperial Institution*, Chicago, London, 1966.

VALJAVEC, F., *Geschichte der deutschen Kulturbeziehungen zu Südosteuropa* (History of Germany's cultural relations with south-eastern Europe), vols. 1–4, Munich, 1953–1965, (vol. 5 in course of publication), (*Südosteuropäische Arbeiten*, nos. 41–45).

JORGA, N., *La Révolution française et le sud-est de l'Europe* (The French Revolution and south-eastern Europe), Bucharest, 1934.

THIERFELDER, F., *Ursprung und Wirkung der französischen Kultureinflüsse in Südosteuropa* (Origins and effects of French cultural influences on south-eastern Europe), Berlin, 1943.

KRETSCHMAYR, H., *Geschichte von Venedig* (History of Venice), vols. 1–3, Gotha, Stuttgart, 1905–1934, reprinted Aalen, 1964.

CESSI, R., *Storia della Repubblica di Venezia* (History of the republic of Venice), vols. 1–2, Milan, 1944–1946.

CESSI, R., *La Repubblica di Venezia e il problema adriatica* (The republic of Venice and the Adriatic problem), Naples, 1953.

THIRIET, F., *La Romanie vénitienne au moyen âge. Le développement et l'exploitation du domaine colonial vénitien (XIIe–XVe siècles)* (Venetian Romania in the middle ages. The development and exploitation of the Venetian colonies), Paris, 1959.

VI

CHURCH HISTORY

HASLUCK, F. W., *Christianity and Islam under the Sultans*, vols. 1–2, Oxford, 1929.

SPINKA, M., *A History of Christianity in the Balkans. A Study in the Spread of Byzantine Culture among the Slavs*, Chicago, 1933.

HADROVICS, L., *Le Peuple serbe et son église sous la domination turque* (The Serbian people and their church under Turkish domination), Paris, 1947.

PAPADOPOULLOS, TH, H., *Studies and Documents Relating to the History of the Greek Church and People under Turkish Domination*, Brussels, 1952 (*Bibliotheca Graeca Aevi Posterioris*, vol. 1).

STADTMÜLLER, G., 'Die Christianisierung Südosteuropas als Forschungsproblem' (Investigation into the conversion of south-eastern Europe to Christianity), *Kyrios*, 6, 1943, pp. 61–102.

VLASTO, A. P., *The Entry of the Slavs into Christendom. An Introduction to the Medieval History of the Slavs*, Cambridge, 1970.

ONASCH, K., *Einführung in die Konfessionskunde der orthodoxen Welt* (Introduction to the different branches of the Orthodox church), Berlin, 1962 (*Sammlung Göschen*, vol. 1197, 1197a).

OBOLENSKY, D., *The Bogomils. A Study in Balkan Neo-Manichaeism*, Cambridge, 1948.

MURKO, M., *Die Bedeutung der Reformation und Gegenreformation für das geistige Leben der Südslaven* (The influence of the reformation and counter-reformation on the spiritual life of the southern Slavs), Heidelberg, 1927.

VII

ECONOMIC HISTORY

GROSS, H., *Südosteuropa. Bau und Entwicklung der Wirtschaft* (Southeastern Europe. Construction and development of the economy), Leipzig, 1937.

STOIANOVICH, T., 'The Conquering Balkan Orthodox Merchant', *Journal of Economic History*, 20, 2 (1960), pp. 234–313.

BUSCH-ZANTNER, R., *Agrarverfassung, Gesellschaft und Siedlung in Südosteuropa. Unter besonderer Berücksichtigung der Türkenzeit* (The agrarian constitution, society and settlers in south-eastern Europe, with special reference given to the period of Turkish rule), Leipzig, 1938.

ZALESKI, E., *Les Courants commerciaux de l'Europe danubienne au cours de la première moitié du XXme siècle* (The trends and policies in the Danubian states during the first half of the twentieth century), Paris, 1952.

SPULBER, N., *The Economics of Communist Eastern Europe*, Cambridge, Mass., 1957.

SANDERS, I. T. (ed.), *Collectivization of Agriculture in Eastern Europe*, Lexington, 1958.

Südosteuropa-Schriften (Southeast-European writings):
   vol. 2, *Wirtschaft und Gesellschaft Südosteuropas. Gedenkschrift für Wilhelm Gülich* (Trade and society in south-eastern Europe. Memorial to Wilhelm Gülich), Munich, 1961.
   vol. 4, *Wirtschaftswissenschaftliche Südosteuropa-Forschung. Grundlagen und Erkenntnisse* (Economic studies of south-eastern Europe. Principles and knowledge), Munich, 1963.

INDEX

War I, 148; supports a 'greater
Serbia', 151; treaty of (1920), 153;
and World War II, 164, 171;
murder of Radić, 166; Red Army
occupy, 171; Bulganin and Khrush-
chev visit, 175
Belisarius, 40
Berat, 95
Berchtold, count von, 147
Berlin, Congress of 1878, 113, 133,
135, 136
Bessarab family, 102
Bessarabia, 112, 131, 138, 163
Bessi, 32
Bihać, 169
Bismarck, 113, 129, 133
Bitolj, 20
Black Hand, the, 145–7
Black Sea, 15, 20, 45, 82
Bled, 175
Bleiburg, massacre of, 174
Bodin, Constantine, 68, 83
Boeotia, 85
Bogdan, 82, 102
Bogomils, Bogomilism, 27, 60, 83
Boleron, Theme of, 49
Boniface of Montferrat, 75
Boril, 75–6
Boris II, tsar of Bulgaria, 61
Boris III, tsar of Bulgaria, 149, 160
Boris-Michael (khan Boris), prince of
Bulgaria, 50, 52, 53, 54
Bosna river, 16, 18, 21, 23, 83
Bosnia, Dinaric Alps in, 15; communi-
cations, 21; mining, 25; religion,
27, 60, 83; unification of tribes, 47,
68; ruled by Tomislav, 65; trade,
79; and Stefan Uroš II, 79; ruled by
Časlav and Kresimir, 83; and
Hungarian domination, 83–5; Tur-
kish advance on, 89; conquered by
Turks, 92–4; annexed by Austria,
113, 137, 140, 145; occupied by
Austria-Hungary, 131, 133; Serbs

migration to, 116; uprising of 1875,
129–30, 132; Russian occupation,
132; Serbian claims in, 135; and
incorporation into Serbia, 138;
land reforms, 157; World War II,
165, 171
Bosphorus, 73
Botev, Christo, 130, 132
Brač (Brazza), 97, 165
Braila, 131
Branimir, prince, 64
Branković, George, 47, 91, 92
Branković, Vuk, 47, 82, 89, 90
Brătianu, Dinu, 171
Brătianu, Ionel, 150
Bratislava, see Pressburg
Brazza, see Brač
Brenner pass, 150
Brindisi (Brundisium), 20
Brod, 21
Broz, Josip, see Tito
Brskova, 79
Brussa (Bursa), 13, 80, 88, 93
Bucharest, 107, 118, 127, 131, 132,
154; treaty of 1812, 112, 113, 126;
treaty of 1913, 142; convention of
1877, 133
Budua (Budva), 16, 98, 99
Bug river, 13, 19, 112
Bukovica, 16
Bukovina, 11, 102, 150
Bulganin, Nikolai Aleksandrovich,
175
Bulgaria, size of population, 11, 156;
rivers, 17; languages, 24; Arnaut
settlements in, 26; religion, 27, 28,
54, 60, 62, 107, 108, 131–2; and
Methodius' disciples, 56; rebellion
of 931, 67; Second Bulgarian
Empire, 68, 72–3, 86; becomes
independent state, 72–86; rebirth
of nationalism, 118–19; education,
119; liberation movement, 131–6;
Bulgarian outrage against Turks,

INDEX

communications, 16, 17, 20–1, 34–5, 138
communism, 170–6
Comneni dynasty, 71, 87
Constantine I, king of Greece, 148
Constantine I, emperor, 37
Constantine IV, emperor, 45
Constantine V Copronymus, emperor, 50
Constantine VII Porphyrogenitus, emperor, 43–5, 59
Constantine, bishop of Preslav, 60
Constantinople, communications, 20; founding, 36; Avar-Slav siege of, 41, 43; Arab sieges of, 48; Bulgarian sieges of, 50, 59; Magyars siege of, 58; Basil II triumphant return to, 62; imprisonment of Stefan Vojslav, 67; Italian conquest of, 71; Ivan Asen, 76–7; Alexius Strategopoulos enters, 77–8; and Stefan Dušan, 81; Turkish conquest of, 88, 92, 107; Turks siege of, 91; the Phanar, Phanariot supremacy in Moldavia and Wallachia, 107; Bulgarian communities in, 118, 131; see also Byzantium, Istanbul
constitution 158–61
Corfu, 78, 147; declaration of, 151, 159, 165
Cosmas, 60
Cossacks, 111
Craiova, treaty of 1940, 163
Cres, see Chesso
Crete, 16, 61, 99, 129, 140
Crimea, 40, 111, 112, 113, 128
Crnojevići family, 96
Croatia, culture in, 22; and Habsburgs, 26, 100–1, 145; religion, 27, 64; Hungarian advances on, 58; clashes with Bulgaria, 60; foundation of independent Croatia, 64–5; acquired by Hungary, 66–7; attacks Venetian shipping, 69; Hungary

regains from Byzantium, 72; Hungarian domination, 83–5; and the reformation, 108; birth of nationalism, 119–21; Ustaša movement in, 163; and World War II, 165–6, 167
Croats, 47, 50, 55, 62, 64
Crusades, 20, 64, 68, 71, 73, 87–8, 91
cultural patterns, 21–2, 28, 60, 107–8
Cumans, 64, 72, 73, 86
Cuza, Alexander, 128
Cvetković, 164, 166
Cvijić, Jovan, 21
Cynoscephalae, battle of, 32
Cyprus, 99
Cyril, 53, 54, 60, 64
Czechoslovakia, 150, 154, 162
Czernowitz (Chernovtsy), 13, 19, 150

Dacia, 34, 35, 37, 39, 40, 41
Dacia Trajana, 35
Dalmatia, Romans in, 23, 24, 34; and Diocletian, 35; Slav races settle in, 45, 50; boundary of Byzantium and Frankish empires, 55; Hungarian advances on, 58; religion, 64; Franks overthrown in, 64; theme of, 65; under Venice, 66, 70; Hungary regains from Byzantium, 72; under Serbian rule, 80; Hungarian domination, 83; collapse of Venetian supremacy in, 97; Venice regains her territories in, 98; literature, 100; influence of Renaissance humanism on, 108; and treaty of Campo Formio, 119; see also Illyria
Dalmatinac, Juraj, 109
Danilo I Petrović, prince-bishop of Cetinje, 127
D'Annunzio, Gabriele, 150–1
Danube (Ister) river, geography of, 16, 17; and communications, 20, 21; name, 23; and Roman empire, 23, 34, 36–7, 40, 41, 42–3; towns on, 25; and Dacian empire, 34; and the

197

INDEX

Rovine, battle of, 89, 90, 102
Rudnik, 79
Rumelia, 105, 135, 136
Russia, rise to power, 110, 113; and support for Montenegro, 116; cultural influence on Bulgaria, 119; and the Orthodox Church, 123–4; and Serbian independence, 126, 127; and Montenegro's independence, 128; and the Bosphorus, 129; declares war on Turkey, 130–3; tension with Great Britain, 131; gains in Bessarabia, 131; joins Bulgaria against Turkey, 132–3; policy towards Bulgaria, 135–6; Serbia allied to, 137; war with Japan, 140; and the Balkan alliance, 141; withdrawal from Balkan affairs, 148; see also Kiev, Moscow, Soviet Union, Sviatoslav
Ruthenia, 150

Šabac, 124
Saif-ad-Daulah, emir, 61
St. Mark, republic of, 119
Salians, 47
Salonica (Thessalonike), roads, 20, 21; Avars besiege, 43; Slav tribes settle near, 46; Theme of, 49; captured by Arabs, 59; Norman occupation, 72, 73; Kalojan besieges, 75; falls to Michael and Theodore Angelus, 77; Zelots in, 80; Wallachian settlers, 86; Turkish conquest, 91; acquired by Venice, 97, 98; Slav population predominant, 139; Turkish officers conspire in, 140; Greece gains, 142; allied troops land in, 148; conferences held at, 154; Germany offers to Yugoslavia, 164
Salzburg, 51, 52
Samo, 45
Samuel, prince of Bulgaria, 87

San Stefano, treaty of 1878, 113, 133, 135
Sanjak railway, 141
Šar Planina, 16
Sarajevo, 12, 18, 21, 93, 114, 134, 141, 145–7
Sava, St., see Rastko-Sava
Sava river, 12, 16, 18, 20, 21, 23, 38, 44, 51, 84, 101, 110, 119, 125, 134, 146,
Schmaus, A., 21
Schönbrunn, treaty of 1809, 119
Scleros, Bardas, 62
Scutari, 16, 34, 86, 95, 98, 125, 134, 143, 146
Scutari, lake, 67
Scythians, 32
Sebastopol, 113
Sebenico (Šibenik), 97
Second Bulgarian empire, 68, 72–3, 86
Selim II, sultan, 99
Selim III, sultan, 128
Seljuks, 62, 71, 87
Semendria, see Smederevo
Senj, 16, 101
Serbia, mining, 25; Arnaut settlements, 26; religion, 27, 28, 74, 107, 108; battles with Bulgaria, 60; becomes independent state, 72–86; Bulgarian influence on succession, 76; war of independence of 1804, 115; nationalism, 117–18; language, 118; granted autonomy, 127; declares war on Turkey, 130; and San Stefano treaty, 133; alliance with Habsburgs, 135; and incorporation of Herzegovina, 138; claims Macedonia, 138–9; and Austrian annexation of Bosnia and Herzegovina, 140–1, 145; treaty with Bulgaria of 1912, 141–2; and Bucharest treaty of 1913, 142; prevents Bulgaria taking Macedonia,

208

INDEX

Zeravna, 106
Zeta, 23, 67, 72, 73, 82, 116; *see also*
Dioclea, Montenegro
Žiča, 74
Zoe, 59
Zog I, king of Albania, 162, 172

Zographou, 118
Zrinski (Zrinji), Peter, 120
Zrmanje river, 16
Župans, 72
Zvonimir, Demetrius, 66, 68
Zvonimir, Helen, 66